BEFORE YOU HIT THE WALL

Danny Lehmann

YWAM
Publishing
A Ministry of Youth With A Mission
P.O. Box 55787, Seattle, WA 98155

Acknowledgements

Special Thanks To:

- Youth With A Mission's frontline missionaries, whose response to these teachings at their Frontier Missions Conference in Thailand prompted me to put them on paper.

- Gordon MacDonald, who helped me "order my private world."

- Mark Buckley, who loved me enough to tell me to slow down.

- Pastors Garry Ansdell, Mike Kiley, Bill Stonebraker, and Chuck Smith, for giving me the Word.

- Geoff Benge, for his labor of love in editing the manuscript, and for his work on Chapter 10.

- Debbie McMillan, my faithful Canadian secretary, who typed the manuscript and picks up the pieces.

- Francis Anfuso, for the title on Chapter 4.

Dedication

To my wife Linda,

Whose constant encouragement to me before and after I've hit The Wall has kept me in the race, and at whose urging this book was born.

Foreword

Danny Lehmann is one of my favorite writers. He is inspiring, practical, and down to earth. He deals with life's real issues.

Before You Hit the Wall identifies one of the most perplexing challenges to all believers. It is a challenge to the disciplined life, not just in the sense of a monk who retreats to a monastery and prays eight hours a day, but a discipline that affects our tongue, eating habits, thought life, rest and recreation, friendships, family life, and most important of all, our passion for God.

To be quite honest, I dread books about self-discipline. I avoid them like the plague—that is one thing I am disciplined in!

You do not need to fear this book. It will not heap condemnation on you, nor will it leave you feeling overwhelmed with all that you have to do to be a disciplined Christian.

Danny shares honestly from his failures. He makes discipline seem not only practical, but possible. He inspires you from his own life, and makes you want to make the hard choices. Not only that, it is based firmly on God's Word. You will be inspired as Danny shares God's Word in ways you thought it never applied.

I read a lot of books, and this one challenged me more than most. I know it will challenge you, as well. Whether you are a leader, new Christian, or have known the Lord for years, you will want to read this book.

Floyd McClung
Amsterdam, Holland
March, 1991

Contents

Do you not know that in a race all the runners run, but only one gets the prize? Run in such a way as to get the prize. Everyone who competes in the games goes into strict training. They do it to get a crown that will not last; but we do it to get a crown that will last forever. Therefore I do not run like a man running aimlessly; I do not fight like a man beating the air. No, I beat my body and make it my slave so that after I have preached to others, I myself will not be disqualified for the prize.

I Corinthians 9:24-27

BEFORE YOU HIT THE WALL

Chapter One

Ouch! Where Did That Wall Come From?

I had been warned about hitting "The Wall," but it was not of great concern to me as I lined up at the start of my first marathon race. The starter's gun cracked and we were off, the 26.2 mile (42 kilometer) race would separate the men from the boys, the well-prepared from the unprepared. I thought I was prepared. Although I'd never run the full distance of a marathon before, I had been running about eight miles a day in training, with an occasional thirteen mile run thrown in.

I could feel the benefits of that training as I ran confidently in the early stages of the race. Finally, I settled into an even pace in the middle of the field of runners, and things progressed well—until the eighteenth mile. Eighteen miles out in my first marathon, I hit The Wall!

At first I thought I was going to die. My body screamed at me, "I hate it, I've had enough, you've abused me too long. I'm quitting!" My training had put my body in shape for a ten kilometer (6.2 mile) race—perhaps, but definitely not a marathon. I no longer cared about the race. All I could think was that if I "bought the farm" (died), my misery would be over. I began looking along the roadside to find a suitable bush to crawl under to die. But before I found my bush, I spotted two girls helping another unfortunate runner who had hit The Wall at the same time I did. The two girls had dragged him to the side of the road, where he sat, crying. My ego wasn't about to let two girls do the same for me, so I plodded on despite the pain. To my surprise, after about ten minutes, I found my "second wind," which allowed me to finish the race.

At the end of the race, I discovered that I had lost six toenails, looked ten years older, and was unable to walk up steps for five days, but I had learned two valuable lessons. I learned, firstly, that I had suffered the pain of hitting The Wall needlessly through my lack of training. Secondly, I learned that there are two choices you can make when you hit The Wall—keep on going, regardless, or drop out of the race.

What does it mean to hit The Wall? Hitting the Wall refers to a point in a marathon, somewhere between the sixteenth and twentieth miles, when your body begins to "run out of gas" and has to "switch tanks."

Glycogen, a glucose producing substance in muscle tissue, builds up in an athlete's body during training. During the race, the body burns the glycogen to supply energy. However, as the supply of glycogen is depleted, the body switches from burning glycogen to burning body fat for energy. When an athlete has worked his body into proper condition, the pain (and I mean pain!) of hitting The Wall is almost nil. But if the athlete has neglected his training, he can expect to hit The Wall—hard!

Many times, the Bible compares the Christian life to a race (Ps. 119:32; Isa. 40:31; Acts 20:24; I Cor. 9:24-25; Gal. 5:7; Phil. 3:14; Heb. 12:1-3). But the Christian life is no hundred meter dash, it's a long-distance endurance race—a marathon. As long as we are on this earth, we're running in the race. Christians are reborn to run, to press on toward the goal that is God's preordained destiny for our lives.

Endurance, the ability to keep on going when others have dropped out, is an essential, although overlooked, quality of both the physical and the spiritual race. There is scarcely an example in the Bible where great men and women of faith did not have to endure many hardships and obstacles in order to achieve God's purpose in their lives.

God is a source of endurance (Rom. 15:5). He could be called the God of endurance. Jesus said that through endurance, we would gain our lives (Luke 21:19). The apostle Paul tells us that he was strengthened through endurance (Col. 1:11), that his ministry was approved through endurance (II Cor. 6:4), that endurance is the first sign of an apostle (II Cor. 12:12), and that tribulation produces endurance in our lives (Rom. 5:3).

The writer to the Hebrews says that endurance is needed in order to obtain God's promises (Heb. 10:36). James tells us that the testing of our faith produces endurance, and that endurance is the key to being a happy person (James 1:3; 5:11).

Paul endured misunderstanding, loneliness, betrayal, physical hardship, persecution, evil doers, and unanswered prayer (II Tim. 2:9; 4:9,10,13,14,20), yet went on to finish his race with joy (II Tim. 4:8). It is the same for us today. God wants to build endurance into our character, and uses trials, testings, Satan's attacks, and even our own self-imposed discipline to this end.

It is always sad to see an athlete who has dropped out of a race while it is in progress. Any of us who read sports magazines or have watched the Olympic Games on television have seen the anguished looks on the faces of athletes who have dropped out. Sometimes they have been forced to drop out because another runner accidentally tripped them, or spiked them in the back of the leg. Sometimes they are forced out because of a lack of training, which makes it impossible for them to keep up the pace. Whatever the reason, it is a sorry sight to see an athlete's dream of running well enough to experience the thrill of victory shattered.

Tragically, there are many today who have dropped out of the Christian life, and who now sit shattered, brokenhearted, and disillusioned at the side of the track, bitter at the circumstances which caused them to drop out of the race.

Yes, the Christian life also has its Wall, and every Christian will encounter it at some point or another. If we are not properly prepared for this encounter with The Wall, it may well cause us to drop out of the race. But, like a well-trained athlete, if we have properly prepared ourselves, the negative effects of hitting The Wall will be reduced, if not obliterated, by God's power.

Becoming a Christian is a joyous affair. We are full of excitement over all that God has done in our lives. Hope and expectation fill our hearts for what lies ahead in our newfound relationship with the Lord and with other people. We are so taken up in the excitement of the moment that all our problems and hassles seem to pale into insignificance.

Then one day, sooner or later, we wake up and find that not everything is new. Many of the old problems and hassles are still there, and need to be dealt with. We discover that the people who used to bug us still do. Worse yet, we have opened ourselves to a whole new category of people who bug us or who fail to meet our expectations—other Christians.

If that weren't enough, we have inherited a supreme enemy—His Satanic Majesty—who will come after us with the vengeance of a spurned lover. Our joy begins to wane in the face of these pressing realities, and we become conscious of the effort needed to live the Christian life. We still feel forgiven and set free in our hearts, but as we face more and more trials, tribulations, temptations, and problems, we begin to have doubts about God's character. Here is where we encounter The Wall.

Some learn to exist under this load, others find it more and more difficult, and eventually drop out of the Christian life. There are still others who groan and grumble to God and to other Christians about their lot. They, in turn, become a brick in The Wall that other Christians will eventually confront in their race.

But there is also another category of Christians: those who encounter these same things, but seem unfazed by them. Somehow, despite all the difficulties they face, they continue to draw spiritual strength and keep on going. These are the people who have worked themselves into proper spiritual condition.

Any of us who grew up watching Saturday morning cartoons has seen the fox. Regardless of his schemes to get past the obstacles and get at the chickens, he always runs headlong into the obstacle. Many Christians are like this in their spiritual lives. They stand beaten and battered, teeth knocked out, stars circling their bruised heads, looking for another way they can try to get over, under, around, or through The Wall.

The point *after* your collision with The Wall, though, is not the time to start looking for a way through it. The key is to anticipate The Wall and plan for it so that it won't knock you spiritually senseless every time you approach it.

No runner who expects to finish a marathon would attempt it without first having a strategy for running the race. A marathon is a very long race, and there are many psychological and physical obstacles to be overcome along the way. Thus, we do not run the marathon as we would the hundred meter dash. Our strategy must sustain us throughout the grueling length of the race. It must anticipate the problems and factor them in to ensure that we have enough reserve energy left to make a strong finish. Those who enter a marathon without such a strategy will rarely finish the race.

What is the most important component in any effective strategy for running the marathon? Training. A runner who has not trained hard and worked himself into peak condition will be lucky to cross the finish line.

"...Exercise thyself rather unto godliness" (I Tim. 4:7 KJV), the Apostle Paul urged his young protege, Timothy. It was wise counsel about the conditioning necessary for the Christian life, from a man who had much experience at living it. Timothy was to train his soul for the purpose of godliness.

Paul knew that Joseph had hit The Wall in Egypt several times. King David had hit The Wall following a fatal attraction to his next door neighbor's wife. The valley of Ono was where Nehemiah hit The Wall, while Jonah managed to hit it in the belly of a whale! In the Garden of Gethsemane, Jesus, too, had come up against The Wall.

Paul experienced more than one encounter with The Wall (see II Cor. 11:23-28). Thus, from the place of Spirit-inspired wisdom, apostolic authority, and many years of experience running in the Christian race, he instructed Timothy to get himself spiritually in shape, because there's trouble coming, and it's spelled with a capital "T."

Eyes on the Prize

To the Corinthians, Paul wrote: "Do you not know that in a race all the runners run, but only one gets the prize? Run in such a way as to get the prize. Everyone who competes in the games goes into strict training. They do it to get a crown that will not last; but we do it to get a crown that will last forever. Therefore I do not run like a man running aimlessly; I do not fight like a man beating the air. No, I beat my body and make it my slave so that after I have preached to others, I myself will not be disqualified for the prize" (I Cor. 9:24-27).

The Corinthians were Greeks, so they understood Paul's meaning. Using the imagery of Olympic-style games, Paul was challenging them to run the spiritual race with gusto. If Paul were saying the same thing in the language of today, he'd probably say something to the effect of, "Look, you guys, if these pagans go through all this self-denial and rigorous training just to win a wreath of dying leaves held together with a piece of fishing line, then how much more should we train with diligence to obtain God's crown for us?"

There are two issues implicit in these verses. The first is the value of the prize. Paul exhorts the Corinthians to be diligent to maintain the proper perspective on the infinitely greater value of God's high calling on their lives when compared with earthly pursuits.

Jesus used value comparisons when relating the parable of the treasure hidden in a field and the parable of the pearl merchant. He used these comparisons as object lessons in explaining the Kingdom of God to His disciples.

The treasure hidden in the field was worth more to the man than all his possessions, so he sold them and bought the field. The "pearl of great price" was worth so much to the pearl merchant that he sold all of his other pearls in order to purchase the one of greater value (Matt. 13:44-45 KJV). According to Hebrews 11:26, Moses "...regarded disgrace for the sake of Christ as of greater value than the treasures of Egypt, because he was looking ahead to his reward."

The second issue implicit in the verses is the proper means for obtaining the prize—strict training (I Cor

9:25). In I Corinthians 9:27, Paul tells us: "...I beat my body and make it my slave so that...I...will not be disqualified for the prize." The Greek word Paul uses for *beat* is *hupopiazo*, which literally means "to give a black eye to." In describing the rigors to which he subjected his flesh, Paul uses the word *doulagogeo*, which means "to bring into slavery."

Some may already be thinking, "Now wait a minute, this is a bit extreme. What about living the abundant life?" However, before we judge Paul too harshly, let's go back to the first issue we raised—the value of the prize.

Are we seeing the glorious spiritual riches that await us as we "discipline ourselves unto godliness"? Are we aware of the rigorous training regimes to which non-Christians subject themselves in pursuit of a corruptible crown of fame, fortune, and flesh? Most importantly, are we seeing that if we fail to discipline ourselves unto godliness, we will naturally become ungodly?

Let me illustrate. Larry was a young man who worked with our ministry in Honolulu. Recently, he had made himself conspicuous by his absence from our prayer meetings and Bible studies. I called Larry into my office and inquired about the reason for his lack of attendance. "I'm going through a dry spell," Larry informed me.

I spent time counseling him and trying to encourage him in his walk with the Lord. I explained to him about the need to discipline ourselves for godliness, and how imperative it is that we do so to "run a good race" and "finish the course" (Acts 20:24) of the Christian life in order to receive our prize. Larry left, promising to ponder what I had told him.

Alas, I had to call Larry back to my office a few weeks later. This time, his spiritual pulse was even harder to find. Instead of training and disciplining himself for godliness, Larry had taken the easy road, turning to the false comforts of entertainment, food, and drink. Without even realizing it, Larry had opened the door to ungodliness by allowing things other than the Comforter to be his source of comfort (John 14:26 KJV).

Larry is typical of so many Christians today. They are like a man crawling through a desert, dying of thirst. He knows that over the next hill is an oasis, resplendent with palm trees, cool water, and fresh fruit. But instead of gathering his remaining strength and disciplining himself to crawl up and over the hill to the oasis, he crawls in the opposite direction out across the flat desert sand. In the mirage of his mind, he finds it "easier."

But the truth is, God's desire is to give us the energy to make it over the hill. All He wants is for us to commit to the task. Larry was caught in a vicious cycle in which many of us find ourselves at some time or another. We are spiritually "dry," because we are not spending time with the Lord. This in turn makes us more spiritually dry, and because we feel so dry, we have less of a desire to spend time with the Lord. It's a downward spiral that has forced many aspiring Christians from the race and disqualified them from the prize. The only way to counter it is to discipline ourselves to godliness and fight our way upward.

Disciplines of the Race

In running a marathon, there are a number of disciplines we must master if we are to go the distance and do well.

What are these disciplines? There is the discipline of weight training and stretching to reduce the risk of injury; the discipline of running sprints to build up speed, and long-distance runs to build stamina and endurance in our bodies. Then there is the discipline of pacing ourselves, so that we don't burn ourselves out in the first few miles of the race. These are called "disciplines," because that is what is needed to apply them.

It takes discipline and determination to crawl out of bed every morning before the sun, or anyone else, is up, and undertake a strenuous exercise regime. It takes discipline in the evening, when all you feel like doing is flopping in front of the TV, to get up, go outside, and jog ten or fifteen miles. And it takes discipline, after the starter's gun has fired, not to streak ahead, but to pace yourself and allow others to run ahead of you.

If we follow these disciplines, they will carry us through the race. When we approach that point of the race where most runners hit The Wall, its effects upon us will be minimal, because we have conditioned our bodies for the race, paced ourselves, and conserved some of our energy.

Then, when we approach the finish line and the prize, we are able to increase our pace and move past runners ahead of us. When we stand on the platform to receive our prize, all the effort that went into practicing the disciplines of marathon running will have been worth it.

The Christian life has its disciplines, too. They are disciplines that, when practiced consistently and properly, will guide us along the course of the Christian life to the finish line and the prize that awaits us.

What are these disciplines? They are the disciplines of the Quiet Time, of Bible Reading and Study, Fasting, Solitude, Rest, Scripture Meditation and Memorization, and yes, Bodily Discipline.

Each one is important, and throughout the remainder of this book, we will look more closely at each of them, so that we can apply them in our lives and run a good race.

Chapter Two

Holes and Goals

"Woe to the man who has to learn his principles in a time of crisis."   Ray Stedman

Before I start a marathon, I set some goals. I establish a time frame within which I think I can run the
race. I then break the race down into sections, and set
times for those sections.

In this way, I can measure my time for each section
to see if I am on target for reaching my goal. So in the
Christian life, we need to have established goals for
which we are striving, and that are in keeping with our
objective of being godly.

There are holes in the road that can trip us up, slow
us down, or even knock us out of the race, if we are not
aware of them. However, being aware of the holes is
not enough: we need some goals for the road.

Holes in the Road

Hole 1—Discipline does not equal godliness.

Paul charged Timothy to discipline himself to godliness. He didn't mean, however, that discipline equals
godliness, but that we are to discipline ourselves for
the purpose of godliness. We all know people who are
very disciplined, but are far from being godly. Discipline only for discipline's sake is worthless. Only

when attached to a goal which we are striving to attain will discipline be worthwhile. However, our goal, and not our discipline, should be what sets us apart. So, for example, we say that a person is a great athlete, because with the application of discipline to their life, they have achieved their goal.

When Carl Lewis won the hundred-meter sprint at the 1984 Olympics in Los Angeles, the crowd clapped and cheered him and said to each other, "He's a great runner." They didn't say, "What a great man of discipline he is." No, Lewis' goal was to win the race. That's what he did, and that's what he is known for—being a great runner. Certainly many hours of agonizing discipline and training went into preparing himself for that race, but it was just the means to an end.

This may seem simple to many, but I am constantly amazed by the number of Christians who miss this point and confuse discipline with godliness. Discipline does us not one ounce of good if it is not locked onto a goal for which we are striving. Discipline does not equal godly character—it is only a means to achieving godly character.

The key in all of this is the value of the prize. If we value the prize that awaits us at the end of the race, there will be no difficulty in applying discipline in order to achieve it. But the discipline is only the means to the end—attaining the prize.

What is it about discipline that makes us able to attain our goals? Before I began marathon running, I thought 26.2 miles was a long way. It still is! I had to think twice about even driving that far to visit a friend! As I began to train for marathons, I had serious doubts about ever being able to run the full distance of the race. However, as I continued to discipline myself and train for the marathon, I noticed that my mental attitude began to change. I soon began to look forward to the time when I could finally get out and run the race. As I trained, I discovered other side benefits. Not only was my mental attitude changing, but my body was physically changing. My weight, pulse, and blood pressure all went down, and I was better able to handle the stress that came with my ministry responsibilities. Everything from time pressure to jet lag seemed easier to handle.

Why was this so? Because in disciplining myself, I had created an environment in my mind and body where things could change. As I took better care of my body and developed it, it responded to this changed environment, and I began to feel healthier. In feeling healthier, I felt more in control of the situations around me. As I felt healthier and began to see the benefits of training, my attitudes toward the marathon became more positive.

The same is true when we discipline ourselves for godliness. Spiritual discipline creates an environment in which God can work at developing His character in our lives.

As Christians, we do ourselves a great disservice and put ourselves in unnecessary danger when we fail to provide an environment within which God can work in our lives. We surround ourselves with an environment that makes "...provision for the flesh..." (Rom. 13:14), instead of putting ourselves in an environment that makes provision for the Spirit. Putting ourselves in such an environment as this, however, requires spiritual discipline, the kind of discipline Paul was referring to when he addressed Timothy.

Early in my ministry, a young man came to me for counsel. With tears in his eyes, this young man confessed the problem he was having with lust. I questioned him about the problem, and he began to tell me how he constantly filled his mind with X-rated movies and pornographic magazines—he had been making provision for the flesh. This is not to say that he wouldn't have been tempted with lust had he been praying and studying the Word instead of pornography, but the environment this young man had created for himself, through his choices, had made provision for his flesh, and made it that much easier for him to fall. As a result, his spiritual life was in ruins. If we want to avoid this pitfall, we must provide the proper atmosphere within which God can do His work in our lives.

Before entering full-time ministry, I was a cement mason. When I wanted to make a concrete driveway, sidewalk, or steps, I first built forms out of wood. The forms were fashioned in the shape I wanted the concrete to take when it had set. When the forms were made and laid in place, I filled them with concrete. The same is true of our spiritual lives. Through the spiritual disciplines, we build the forms into which God can cement His character in our lives.

In creating such an environment or form, we must remember that discipline is only the means to an end—not the end in itself. Godliness, not discipline, is our goal.

Hole 2—Turning disciplines into laws.

Another hole into which it's easy to fall (especially for the hyper-zealous) is to become legalistic in our approach to spiritual discipline. Setting goals is a part of discipline, but our goals must serve our objective—to know Christ. We must be careful that we don't allow our goals to become instruments of condemnation with which Satan clubs us every time we fail to achieve one of them. Goals are only guides to keep us running confidently on the narrow road toward the prize.

If, for instance, my goal is to read through the Bible in a year, and at the end of that year, I have only read as far as Jeremiah, I must not feel condemned by Satan—or worse yet, myself—for only getting that far.

Instead, I should be rejoicing that I was able to read that far through the Bible.

If your prayer life is virtually nonexistent, and you set the goal of praying a half-hour each day, but, after several months, you find you've only managed to pray for fifteen minutes a day, you should rejoice over the progress you've made, instead of being downcast over not achieving your goal. Condemnation is the one "nation" to which God has commanded us not to go!

In 1988, I set a goal of memorizing the whole book of Romans. My plan was to do it within one year, but it wasn't until 1990 that I finally committed the last verses of the book to memory. Yet I still praise God for His grace. According to my timetable, I didn't reach the goal, but within two years, my objective—knowing Christ through His word—was realized. We must make sure our goals serve us, and that we don't become a slave to our goals.

Beware of legalism, for it sucks the very life and vitality out of our relationship with the Lord.

Hole 3—Comparing ourselves to others.

Paul told the Corinthian Christians that comparing themselves with others was not wise (II Cor. 10:12). Such an observation seems obvious, but if we look at someone who is more disciplined than we are, our natural inclination is to envy the person and feel condemned because we are not as disciplined.

On the other hand, our natural inclination, when we see someone who is less disciplined than we are, is to become self-righteous and proud. Thus, comparing ourselves to others is a no-win situation. Instead of comparing ourselves to others, we need to ask God for His grace, self-control, and discipline as we set the objectives, goals, priorities, and practices that will lead us to godliness.

In all of this, however, don't forget the slogan of a well-known brand of running shoes—"You gotta let

U.B.U.!" Each of us is unique: there is nobody in the world exactly like you. God made us to be unique expressions of His character. Thus we need to allow God to develop in us everything that He created us to be. He doesn't want Christians to be carbon copies of each other, but unique expressions of Him.

I have been to churches where the congregation acts, talks, and walks like the pastor. In their quest for godliness, these people mimic the pastor. Unfortunately, they fail to see that they look like a ridiculous bunch of people playing a sick joke on the pastor. True godliness is developed when we recognize our uniqueness and allow God to develop it. It is "Christ in you, the hope of glory" (Col. 1:27). We need to open up and let His glory radiate out.

There is no one perfect way to run a marathon that every runner should mimic. There are all kinds of variables that determine how a person runs. Some have long legs; others, short legs. Some are tall and slender; others are short and dumpy. All of these things determine how a runner will run. A runner built close to the ground should not try to mimic a tall runner. Thus, every runner must develop his own style.

Neither does it do any good to compare various runners and say a particular runner must be a good runner because he is tall and slender and has a long stride, while another must be a poor runner because he has short legs and is oddly shaped. You tell a good runner, not by comparing him with another runner, but by who crosses the finish line first.

Perhaps the tall, long-legged person we thought was a good runner had not done the necessary training and had been forced to drop out of the race when he hit The Wall. The short, odd-shaped person, on the other hand, may have had an effective running style and had properly prepared himself for the race, so that he was able to get to the front of the field of runners and win the race.

During the 1930s, a runner by the name of Glenn Cunningham was, for a time, the world's fastest mile runner. Glenn Cunningham was different than other runners, however, because as a child, he had lost four of his toes in a fire. He realized his uniqueness, worked to overcome his adversity, and eventually excelled in running. In the Christian life, we should do the same.

It does us no good to compare ourselves to one another. Instead, we should take the energy we often expend on doing this very thing, and apply it to developing godliness in our life and character.

Hole 4—Human willpower.

"Self-control is just controlling yourself. It's listening to your heart, and doing what is smart." So sings a frog in the children's musical, "The Music Machine," based on the fruit of the Spirit from Galatians 5:22. It's crucial to note, however, that self-control is not just natural human willpower. Self-control is a fruit, a by-product of God's Spirit dwelling and working within our lives.

I have discovered, through personal experience and from biblical example, that human effort, self-assertion, positive thinking, and willpower are of little use in the quest for godliness. Throughout my years at elementary school, I was a straight "C" student. I barely squeaked through high school, and was forced to abandon any hopes I had of going to college, because of a lack of discipline. Instead of school, I told my family, "I'm going surfing," and for the next four years, lived the life of a California beach bum, regularly blowing out my brains on drugs.

At age twenty-one, a long-haired, broken, burned-out freak with barely enough discipline to hold down a job, I landed at the foot of the Cross, and was gloriously saved. Since that time, God, through His

mercy and grace, has helped me to discipline my life—
not because I had any natural endowment of stick-to-
itiveness, but because His Holy Spirit came and took
up residence in my life when I surrendered to Him and
trusted Him.

Trust, spelled with a capital "T," is the key. If we want
to better our devotional life, we must trust Him. If we
want to know and love God's Word better, we must
trust Him, and not our human willpower. If we want
to be able to say "no" to people and food in order to
spend solitary time with God fasting and meditating,
we must trust Him. All of God's dealings with man—
Christian and non-Christian—are for one purpose: to
bring us to a point where we will trust Him.

We must never forget the Lord's charge to Zerub-
babel, "'Not by might nor by power, but by my Spirit,'
says the Lord Almighty" (Zech. 4:6).

Goals for the Road

Having become aware of some of the holes that
could easily trip us up, we now need some goals as we
set out to run the course of the Christian life.

Goal 1—Find God's objectives.

Our objective is our long-range goal. It is where we
want to go. God's objective for Paul was that he obtain
the "...prize of the high calling of God...." Thus the
goals he set for himself to achieve this objective were
buffeting his body, bringing it into slavery to Christ,
and forgetting those things which were behind him
(Phil. 3:10-14; I Cor. 9:27 KJV). Paul's objectives kept
his actions focused and headed in the right direction.

In each of the spiritual disciplines under discussion, we need to be focused as to where we are going
with them. Thus, our objective becomes the "plumb
line" by which we ensure that our subsequent goals,
priorities, and practices are in line and on target. This
is crucial lest we fall into legalism and condemnation

on the one hand, and foggy, unfocused activity on the other.

In my life, I have found that God emphasizes different things at different times. Sometimes He will be emphasizing my need to focus on meditation and solitude, while at other times He will emphasize Bible study and prayer, and still other times, extended periods of fasting. It is important, then, that we are led by the Holy Spirit in determining the particular objective God has for us at a certain point or "season" of our life.

Goal 2—Set attainable goals.

Goal-setting is in vogue these days, especially within management circles. But goal-setting is also very apparent in the Bible. Noah had a goal of building an ark. Nehemiah had a goal of rebuilding the wall of Jerusalem. Jesus has a goal—of seeing the whole world evangelized!

Despite this, within Christianity today, we often fall into a pitfall of setting goals without objectives. As an example, witness the number of Christians who go off to college to earn a degree. They have little understanding about why they need one, the kind of degree God wants them to get, or how He wants them to use it after college. As Christians, we must redeem our time, which makes it crucial that we discern God's objectives in all we do, and set goals in keeping with His objectives.

Our goals must have two qualities: they must be attainable, and they must be measurable. They must be attainable, because our human nature is such that we build upon our accomplishments. Thus, setting a goal of going on a forty-day fast when we've never willingly given up a single meal is an unrealistic goal. If we continually set goals for ourselves that are too high, we will soon become discouraged when we fail to meet or maintain them. Setting reachable, attainable goals provides us with a platform upon which we can build. Of course, implied in the word *discipline* is the idea that we not only reach our goal, but that we maintain it on a regular basis, once it has been reached.

Our goals must be measurable so that we can see the progress we are making. An objective is the ultimate end of our pursuit, while a goal is the "measuring marker" with which we can gauge our progress toward reaching our objective. Achieving an unmeasured goal is like shooting an arrow into the wall, then drawing a bull's-eye around it!

Goal 3—Establishing our priorities.

Paul prayed that the Philippians would "...approve things that are excellent..." (Phil. 1:10 KJV). Put another way, Paul is praying that they would set the right priorities. Once we have established our objectives and set attainable, measurable goals for achieving them, then we must fix our priorities. This means that we must learn to say "no," not only to the world, the flesh, and the devil, but also to the hundreds of other good things that we could do for God, but which will sidetrack us from attaining our objective. There is only one "...good, and acceptable, and perfect, will of God" (Rom. 12:2 KJV) for our lives. Our task is to find it and pursue it with all our might.

Several of my friends are teaching pastors, and they have had to learn to say "no" to much of the counseling, administration, and visitation that needs to be done, in order to give themselves the time they need to study and pray. In turn, they can effectively carry out the ministry to which God has called them. Bible teaching is their top priority. Likewise, in the face of a social crisis in the church, the apostles gave themselves to the Word of God and prayer (Acts 6:1-7). They delegated others to take care of the pressing matters at hand, so they could focus on the objectives God had established for them. In the face of tremendous human need, Jesus often said "no," choosing to set a higher priority on spending time with the Father in prayer.

Goal 4—Practice the disciplines.

At the risk of sounding redundant, before you set your alarm clock for 5:00 a.m. tomorrow, spend some unhurried time with the Father. Allow the Spirit to gently guide you in setting your objectives, goals, and priorities. Check your heart for legalism, comparison, human willpower, and unattainable, hyper-idealistic goals. Start out small, like a grain of mustard seed, and watch a life of discipline grow.

Don't become discouraged if you should fail—pick yourself up and keep going. Proverbs tells us that a righteous man falls seven times, but gets back up again (Prov. 24:16). If you should fall into a hole, climb out and keep going. Most of all, when you hit The Wall, keep on going!

The narrow road to an abundant life of practicing and enjoying the presence of God is before you. The cloud of witnesses of the disciplined saints of the past is cheering you on (Heb. 11:1). The power of God and the fruit of His Holy Spirit are with you.

So...*just do it!*

Chapter Three

Good Morning, Lord

or, Good Lord, It's Morning!

"My number one concern is the care of my
own soul."   Jonathan Edwards

I had just completed a speaking engagement, and
the leader of the missionary training center at which I
had spoken was driving me back to the airport. We
were involved in lighthearted conversation as we
drove along, when suddenly a question popped into
my mind.

"How's your Quiet Time?" I asked.

Immediately, the jovial mood that had filled the car
changed to one of sobriety, as the leader's head sank
in shame.

"To tell you the truth," he confessed, "I haven't had
a decent Quiet Time in months!"

He went on to tell about the enormous demands
that ministry required of him; the time pressure, the
need to make early morning phone calls and send
faxes, decisions to make, meetings to attend, not to
mention spending time with his family.

As I was about to board my plane, this leader,
realizing all he had given me was a string of excuses
for squeezing God out of his life, asked, brokenly and

humility, if I would hold him accountable in the area of his time spent with the Lord. Every time we met in the future, I was to question him about his Quiet Time. I did just that, and today he is a changed man. His face now reflects the joy of the Lord, and not just because he is out from under condemnation about his irregular Quiet Times, but because spending time in the presence of God naturally brings "...fulness of joy..." (Ps. 16:11 KJV).

Since then, I have had many opportunities to interview and talk with Christians regarding their daily Quiet Time with the Lord, and have found that many of them, including pastors and leaders, neglect to spend regular time developing intimacy with God.

How tragic this is when Scripture infers that: 1—God desires relationship, intimacy, and friendship with us (Jer. 9:23-24; John 17:3); 2—Our relationship with God is our most important relationship (Matt. 22:37-39); 3—Intimacy takes time; 4—Any ministry or work we undertake for God is dead work, unless it flows from our relationship with God (Heb. 9:14). Thus, it becomes imperative that we spend time alone in the presence of God. It is our highest priority.

First Things First

Developing an early morning Quiet Time must begin with priority-setting the night before. Some of us are, by nature, "night owls," and others are "morning larks." So, under the spirit of liberty (II Cor. 3:17), we are free to maximize our natural rhythms of effectiveness. However, the weight of Scripture seems to be on the side of an early morning time with God (Ps. 57:8; 63:1; 90:14; 108:2; Prov. 8:17; Isa. 26:9; Mark 1:35).

If we are going to give God the "top of the morning," then we need to discipline ourselves regarding our bedtime at night. This means that late-night work, television, and *Koinonitus* (a disease brought on by overdoses of fellowship!) need to be evaluated in the

light of not only our ability to get out of bed in the
morning and spend time with the Lord, but also our
ability to be fresh and alert during that time.

George Whitefield, who rose every morning at 4:00,
would cease whatever he was doing at 10:00 p.m. and
go to bed. As 10:00 p.m. approached, even in the midst
of fellowship in his own home, he would rise and say,
"Come, gentlemen, it is time for all good folks to be at
home."

This same tenacity is needed during the Quiet Time
as we discipline ourselves to avoid interruptions and
distractions. It seems that every "urgent" phone call,
problem, or emergency will be competing for our time
once we purpose in our heart to spend time with God.
On one occasion, John Knox, the Scottish reformer, was
interrupted from his Quiet Time by a friend incessantly knocking on his door. Knox finally opened the door,
and his friend informed him that the King of England
had come to visit, and was impatient to see Knox. "You
tell the King of England," Knox told his friend, "that I
am meeting with the King of the Universe, and I won't
be interrupted by him!"

Out of the "Ozone"—A Model for Quiet Times

"Spacing-out," or drifting off into the "ozone,"
seems to be the greatest hindrance to an effective Quiet
Time. Spacing-out refers to those times when we are
praying or meditating on the Word of God and our
mind just seems to wander, or we fall asleep. I'm sure
that all of us have experienced this at some point, but
what can we do to avoid it? Psalm 100 has some helpful
insights regarding this subject, insights which have
helped me increase the percentage of times I arise early
from my bed in the morning and say, "Good morning,
Lord," rather than, "Good Lord, it's morning!"

Shout for joy to the Lord, all the earth.
Worship the Lord with gladness;
come before him with joyful songs.

Know that the Lord is God.
It is he who made us, and we are his;
we are his people, the sheep of his pasture.
Enter his gates with thanksgiving
and his courts with praise;
give thanks to him and praise his name.
For the Lord is good and his love endures
for ever; his faithfulness continues through
all generations. (Ps. 100)

Contained in these verses is not only the antidote for spacing-out and drifting off into the ozone, but also a pattern for having an effective Quiet Time.

1—Sing and be joyful. "Shout for joy to the Lord..." (verses 1-2).

Before entering your Quiet Time, simply start to sing. "I don't feel like singing early in the morning. The only thing I feel in the morning is tired!" you say, but nonetheless, these verses instruct us to shout for joy. So, feel like it or not, we must make a deliberate choice and force our will to obey. David prayed, "My heart says of you, 'Seek his face!' Your face, Lord, I will seek" (Ps. 27:8). You'll be amazed at how singing and making a joyful noise to the Lord changes your countenance and wakes you up! But more than this, it also sets the tone for our time with the Lord. It says to the Lord, "I'm here, I'm happy and joyful about being here, let's have fellowship!"

2—Realize who it is you are with. "Know that the Lord is God..." (verse 3).

A few moments of meditation upon God's power ("...It is he who made us, and we are his..."), God's sovereignty ("...we are his people, the sheep of his pasture"), and God's goodness ("For the Lord is good and his love endures forever..." [verse 5]) will greatly help us as we enter our time of fellowship with the Lord.

Meditating upon God in this way moves our focus from us to Him. We are awed by His vast greatness and power, and humbled by the way He loves and cares for each of us. Having seen God as He really is, our focus will be in the right place when we pray and present our petitions to Him. This also helps us to enter in by faith, the essential element in prayer (Heb. 11:6). When we pray, our focus will primarily be on His good pleasure, will, and kingdom, instead of focusing on us and our needs.

The disciples understood this principle. When faced with persecution from the Sadducees, they first confessed the Lord's power, saying, "...Lord...you made the heaven and the earth and the sea, and everything in them" (Acts 4:24). Then they focused on His sovereignty, quoting Old Testament prophecies (Acts 4:25-28). Only after they had acknowledged God's rightful place did they ask for His goodness and mercy (Acts 4:29-30).

A proper understanding of God's goodness and mercy is crucial. Goodness and mercy are the aspects of God's character which allow us to trust Him as Our Father. He is a Father who desires our highest good, so we do not need to be worried that He will step on us to accomplish His sovereign will.

3—Begin the time with thanksgiving. "Enter his gates with thanksgiving..." (verse 4).

After singing to the Lord, praising Him for who He is, and meditating upon attributes of His character, we need to thank God specifically for all the things He has done for us. Remembering past deeds God has done in our behalf reinforces our faith for the future. The Lord told the Israelites to remember His delivering power by heaping up stones of remembrance (Josh. 4, I Sam. 7:12).

The various Hebrew feasts (Passover, Pentecost, Tabernacles, and the like) were intended by God as

reminders to the Jewish people of His past faithfulness
to them. We are commanded throughout Scripture to
have a thankful heart (Eph. 5:20; Phil. 4:6; Col. 2:7; 3:15;
4:2; I Thess. 5:18), and being ungrateful is seen as a
mark of ungodliness (Rom. 1:21; II Tim. 3:2; Luke
17:11-19).

I often fill up a section of my prayer diary with both
the big and the little things for which I am thankful. If
I have difficulty thinking of somewhere to begin, I start
by thanking the Lord for my body. "Lord, I thank You
for my hair, my mind, my eyes, ears, nose, mouth,
tongue, lungs, vocal chords, skin, arms, fingers, my
neurological system, circulatory system, digestive and
reproductive systems, my blood, legs, feet, and toes."
Sometimes I go on to thank the Lord for my health, my
wife, and my two beautiful sons. Other times, I thank
God for the incarnation of Christ, the Cross, the Resur-
rection...my Bible, the mission with which I serve, my
church, my pastors, and the like. When you think
about it, there are hundreds of things that God has
done for us on which we can focus and for which we
can thank Him. A few moments spent each day
recounting our daily blessings helps us look forward
to spending time with the "lover of our souls" in the
intimacy of our daily Quiet Time.

4—Praise Him. "...and [enter] his courts with
praise" (verse 4; Eph. 5:19).

Time spent thanking the Lord for all He has done
for us is sure to put us in the mood for praising and
worshiping Him. From my experience, a time of praising and worshiping God is a time of spontaneity and
intimacy. Often during these times, I sing psalms to the
Lord.

Hundreds of worship songs have been written by
setting verses from Psalms and other passages of Scripture to music. My friends, David and Dale Garratt,
have taken their "Scripture in Song" choruses around

the world and helped thousands to enter a deeper life of worship. Not only are these songs a great tool for worship and praise to God, but they are also an excellent way to memorize Scripture.

During my Quiet Time, I often sing hymns. I was not raised in an evangelical environment, and became a Christian during the "Jesus Movement" of the early 1970s. I had little exposure to the rich heritage of hymns we have in the Church. One day, however, I purchased several old hymnals and began reading the words to the hymns.

As I read, I was astounded at the depth of understanding and insight about God, His ways, and His character that these hymn writers displayed. I often sing those hymns I know to the Lord during my Quiet Time. Even though my singing does not rival Michael W. Smith or Sandi Patti, God is blessed! I read aloud the hymns I don't know to the Lord, lifting up the words of such great hymn writers as Fanny Crosby, Charles Wesley, and Isaac Watts as praise to the Lord.

There are other times when I sing spiritual songs (Col. 3:16). A spiritual song is a song that wells up from deep inside my heart, and I spontaneously make up the melody and words. To someone listening, such a song may sound disjointed and childish. Be that as it may, it remains a glorious way to express worship from the depths of my spirit.

5—Pray specifically. When, by faith, we are before the throne of grace (Heb. 4:16), we have the liberty to ask God for specific requests. Philippians chapter four lays out a similar pattern for prayer to that found in Psalm 100. After exhorting us to rejoice and be thankful, Paul urges us to present our specific requests to God and, as a result, experience the peace of God (Phil. 4:4-7). In fact, our vague "Thy will be done" prayers are not always honoring to God. It is true that there are times when all we can do is throw up our hands and rest in God's sovereignty, but to do that all the time reflects a lack of faith in His ability to hear and act upon specific prayer petitions.

The weight of scriptural command (Matt. 7:8; 21:22; Luke 11:9; John 14:13; 15:7; 16:24; James 5:14) and example (Neh. 1; Dan. 9; John 17; Acts 12:5; James 5:17) falls on the side of making our specific requests known to God. As we draw closer to Him, we are better able to discern His will in prayer by our knowledge of His word (Dan. 9:2), the leading of the Holy Spirit (Acts 16:6-10), and by the desires of our own heart, if we are truly committed to obeying Him (Ps. 37:4). It is through seeing specific prayers answered that our faith grows, as we see God move people and circumstances on our behalf.

This is the antidote for "spacing out." If we follow this pattern, or a similar one geared to our personal tastes, it will lead us into the presence of God, where we can enjoy intimate fellowship with Him. When we enter into such intimacy with God, our Quiet Time becomes something we long for and look forward to with expectancy. No longer is it a drudgery or "duty" to get out of bed in the morning, it becomes a joy, for we know the great reward of the fellowship and intimacy with God that awaits us.

Quiet Time Accessories

Listed below are several Q.T.A.'s—Quiet Time Accessories—that will aid us as we develop the discipline of a regular Quiet Time with the Lord. Some of the following may seem a little mechanical, but I assume I'm writing to fellow strugglers in developing the discipline of a daily Quiet Time. As you read, ask the Lord to help you "eat the fish and spit out the bones." Assimilate into your life those things which actually help you in developing your Quiet Time; you are under no obligation to rigidly follow every point.

1—A Prayer Diary. There are several different types of prayer diaries available. For the past nine years, I have used the Personal Prayer Diary, published by Youth With A Mission. This diary assigns one Old Testament and one New Testament passage to each day. Reading these daily passages will take you through the Old Testament once and the New Testament twice each year. One nation or unreached people group is assigned to each day so that you can systematically pray throughout the year for the nations of the world and those who have yet to hear the Gospel. Under each day, seven lines are provided for recording your prayer projects.

As I mentioned, this is just one of a number of prayer diaries available, so look around and find the one you are comfortable with, become familiar with it, but most of all, use it.

I like to integrate the use of a prayer diary into my Quiet Time in the following way. I break the seven lines under each day into sections for different aspects of my life that need prayer. On the first line, I record the things I'm thankful for that day. First, I thank God for the specific blessings of the previous day, and then move on to thank Him for more general things such as my salvation, my family, my Bible, my health, my friends, and the like.

On the second line, I enter the word "Character," at which point I pray about areas in my life that need a special touch from God. Perhaps the day before I had been overly irritated at someone, or at some event that happened to me. So beside "Character," I write "anger," and then wait upon the Lord, should He have some Scripture or prophetic word He wants to give to me. If He does, I write it down alongside "anger."

Sometimes at this point, I might deviate and undertake a word study to gain, from a biblical perspective, more understanding about the issue at hand. Having gained this understanding, I can use it in my prayers as I diligently seek victory over that area in my life.

Sometimes I get on my knees to pray, other times I lie with my face to the floor, and still other times I stand. The posture we assume for prayer isn't the crucial thing; the crucial thing is our attitude of heart. Our heart attitude must be one of humility and submission to the Lord.

Often during these times of prayer, I will pray Scripture prayers relating to character as they are recorded in the Psalms, "Create in me a clean heart...Lord, make me to know mine end, and the measure of my days...that I may know how frail I am" (Ps. 51:10; 39:4 KJV). Or I pray the prayers that Paul prayed for the churches as he asked for wisdom, understanding, insight, and endurance for them (Eph. 1:16-19; 3:14-19; Phil. 1:9-11; Col. 1:9-12).

It is also important to acknowledge the good changes God has already wrought in our character. Paul tells us that this will also help us in sharing our faith with others (Phile. 6). By God's grace, we are not only forgiven, but hopefully, we are being changed to be more like Him (Rom. 8:29; II Cor. 3:18). Remember, though, times of praying over problem areas of character weakness are just that. They are not an excuse for a time of self-flagellation, which in turn invites Satan's condemnation.

On the line under "Character," I write "Family," and pray for each member of my family. I am the priest of my home, and as such, am responsible to uphold each member of my family in prayer. I pray for their struggles and their protection. Sometimes I even pray for my boys' future, for their calling, their holiness, and their future wives. If the Lord should give me a special verse or word for them, I write it down and pass it on to them.

Under "Family," I write "Ministry." This is the time when I pray for the various forms of ministry in which I'm involved. If it's evangelism, then I pray that the "...word of the Lord may have free course..." (II Thess. 3:1). If it's teaching or counseling, I pray for wisdom and for the Word to do its powerful work (James 1:5; Isa. 55:11). After "Ministry," I write "Leadership," and pray for those under my leadership—the leaders under me, the staff and students in our training schools, or decisions facing our missionary work.

Following "Leadership," I write the letters "P.E." for Personal Evangelism, and pray for those I've recently witnessed to or led to Christ. I pray against Satan stealing the Word away after it has been sown in a person's heart (Matt. 13:19). I pray also that I may have a greater care and concern for lost souls, that God would give me a revelation of their lost state and a love for them that runs deep enough to tell them the truth of the Gospel, as well as the wisdom to do so effectively (Prov. 11:30).

Finally, on the last line, I write the names of some of my friends. I pray for those who have asked me for prayer, for my backslidden friends, and for those whom God places upon my heart. The Lord restored the fortunes of Job when he had prayed for his friends (Job 42:10).

This is how I use a prayer diary during my Quiet Time. It is a tool which helps me focus my prayers and pray more effectively.

I have kept my used prayer diaries since 1982. They now serve as a record of my prayers, as well as a chronology of my spiritual journey.

For instance, in 1986 and 1987, I went through two very difficult trials, each of which lasted for several months. Both of them are recorded in my prayer diary, so I can see step-by-step how God not only brought me out alive—which I was doubting at the time—but with victory.

I have recorded the insights given by the Lord and the Scripture passages He used to encourage me and bring me through the ordeal. This record of God's dealings with me gives me faith for future times when I'll inevitably hit The Wall again.

You may choose to model your use of a prayer diary on this, or you may choose to develop your own pattern of use. Whatever you decide, a prayer diary is a great asset in developing the discipline of a regular Quiet Time.

2—A Prayer Journal. A prayer journal is different from a prayer diary. My prayer diary is where I record my prayer projects. It's a tool to keep my prayers on track and to encourage my faith when I look back and see the ways in which God has answered my prayers. The things I record in my prayer journal, however, are usually of a much more personal nature.

My prayer journal is where I'm "gut-level" honest with the Lord about my spiritual condition. Some days' entries resemble David's psalms during one of his down times: "My God, my God, why have you forsaken me?...my tongue sticks to the roof of my mouth..." (Ps. 22:1,15). Other entries are full of victorious triumph.

What is important is that in my prayer journal, I articulate what I'm *really* feeling inside. It's where I can be totally honest with God, and writing it down helps me to be honest with myself.

In my prayer journal, I often write out my prayers in longhand. Thus, one morning, while struggling through some trials, I entered the following prayer in my journal: "I feel frustrated lately—time pressure— struggling to be a loving person and not too busy for people, but I'm finding I'm getting irritable, not called—but driven. I need Your grace to sustain me and help me 'finish my course with joy.' I recognize it as a spiritual thing—Satan trying to burn me out. Help me to get victory...."

On another occasion, my journal reads: "I feel a small revival coming on in my spirit. I feel more desire to pray and witness for You, Lord. My family life is good. Your presence seems more real to me. I feel honored and blessed by You in the ministry. The response from the church I spoke at on Sunday and the YWAM schools is humbling. Thanks for the privilege of serving You."

Be wary. It is easy in writing a journal to get hung-up on methods and practices. Don't feel bound to make entries every day, or write a certain amount of words. Start where you are, and allow God to lead you by His Spirit. Neither does a prayer journal need to be a fancy or exquisitely bound book. Mine is just a spiral notebook.

3—A Prayer Closet. "Thus I have beheld Thee in the sanctuary, to see Thy power and Thy glory..." (Ps. 63:2 NASB).

I have found that it helps me greatly to have a physical place (closet, desk, room, etc.) that I can call "my" sanctuary—the place where God and I meet together. I have fixed up a closet in my apartment with a bookshelf, pillow, prayer reminders, and maps on the wall. However, since nearly a third of my time is spent traveling, I have learned to make do with airports, planes, trains, buses, and cars as my sanctuary.

Even so, when I get to the place where I will be staying, I find a sanctuary where I can spend time with the Lord. Sometimes it's on a rooftop or under a tree, other times it's the corner of a library or a chair on a balcony. Occasionally I take a prayer walk, but mostly, I like a physical place where I can go and commune with the Lord.

Other Q.T.A.'s I like to have on hand in my sanctuary are a hymnal, a Bible dictionary, and a concordance, as well as several different translations of the Bible. I also like to have a few standard devotional books on hand. These are helpful, but I would add one caution: don't let revelation from someone else's Quiet Time be a substitute for what you can get directly from the Lord.

A regular Quiet Time is one of the greatest joys we as Christians can enter into with the Lord. However, it takes time and determination to develop. Our natural inclination at 6:00 a.m., when it is dark and cold, is to reach over and switch the alarm off and go back to sleep. It takes a deliberate act to crawl out of bed and spend time with the Lord. However, as you do so, you will begin to experience what the hymn writer meant when he wrote:

There is a place of quiet rest
Near to the heart of God,
A place where sin cannot molest,
Near to the heart of God
O Jesus, blest Redeemer,
Sent from the heart of God,
Hold us who wait before Thee
Near to the heart of God.

Chapter Four

Are You Brainwashed?

or, Is Your Brain Washed?

"This Book will keep you from your sins, or
your sins will keep you from this Book."
                                        Dwight L. Moody

I was a week old in my new faith, and was greatly
confused by the conflicting advice I was getting from
two different groups of Christians. One group, the
group that had led me to Christ, followed the teachings
of a rather mystical Chinese man who taught that Bible
study was unnecessary and a product of the "carnal
mind." Instead, they advocated "pray-reading" the
Scriptures, and chanting the name of the Lord.

The other group of Christians, from Calvary
Chapel in Costa Mesa, California, had given me a set
of thirty of Pastor Chuck Smith's teaching cassettes on
the book of Ephesians. They told me that getting
"grounded in the Word" was my greatest need.

Finally, utterly confused, I went to Jim Westberg (a
converted Jewish Bible teacher) for some counsel. Jim
spoke to me with the authority of a prophet. "Danny,"
he said, "You read and study God's Word. You memorize God's Word. You meditate on God's promises, and
in a few years, you'll have one thing that this mystical
group doesn't have—*and that's answers!*"

I am eternally grateful to Jim Westberg for his wise counsel. His wisdom and understanding saved me from the frustration of building my spiritual house on the sand of human wisdom, mindless chanting, and name repetition, rather than on the solid rock of God's unchanging Word (Matt. 7:21-27).

I began to read and study the Bible. I drank in all Chuck Smith had to say on Ephesians. My appetite for spending time in God's Word was whetted.

Benefits of God's Word

One afternoon, not too long after my talk with Jim Westberg, I was sitting on the 26th Avenue Beach in Santa Cruz, California, reading my Bible. As I read along, one verse seemed to leap off the page at me. "That he might sanctify and cleanse it with the washing of water by the word" (Eph. 5:26 KJV).

Being a young Christian, I totally disregarded the context of the verse, and took it to be God's direct word to me regarding the damage I had done to my mind through four-and-a-half years of drug abuse. (I use the term *abuse* loosely. In reality, the drugs abused *me*. I can't remember a drug that I abused!)

"If you get into My Word, and allow it to do its cleansing work, I'll heal your mind and restore all that has been lost," the Holy Spirit seemed to be impressing on my heart. I followed the impression up by studying other Scripture passages to do with cleansing and restoration (Titus 3:5; Joel 2:25).

I began to study and read the Bible, just as the Holy Spirit had instructed me, and it wasn't long before spending time in the Word and witnessing for Christ were my two greatest passions in life. Today, I am a testimony to the power of God's Word. He has restored my mind. Today I am able to memorize whole books of the Bible. The Lord also has placed me in a position of leadership and has given me responsibilities that I could not have imagined carrying when I was first converted.

As I studied the Bible, I discovered that there are other benefits God offers us when we dig deep into His word.

What are some of these other benefits?

God's Word:

- Saves us (James 1:21)
- Produces faith (Rom. 10:17)
- Regenerates us (James 1:18)
- Nourishes us (I Pet. 2:1-2)
- Guides us (Ps. 119:105)
- Gives us victory over sin (Ps. 119:11)
- Gives us victory over Satan (Eph. 6:17; Luke 4:1-13)
- Makes us holy (John 17:17)
- Is a mirror to our soul (James 1:23; Heb. 4:12)
- Gives us spiritual insight (Ps. 119:130)
- Cleanses us (Eph. 5:26; Titus 3:5)
- Brings us joy (Jer. 15:16)

Given these benefits, we would do well to ask God for the grace to discipline ourselves in studying His word.

From my experience, I have found there are five effective ways to hide God's Word in our heart (Ps. 119:11). They are *reading, studying, hearing, meditating, and memorizing.*

In the pages that follow, we will discuss the first four. We will deal with memorization in the next chapter. Remember, our goal is to develop the practical discipline of spending time in the Word of God.

Reading

"Seek and read from the book of the Lord..."

(Isa. 34:16 RSV).

"...give attendance to reading..."

(I Tim. 4:13 KJV).

Of the four areas we will cover in this chapter, if we were to choose one as the most important, it would certainly be reading. Throughout the Bible, we are exhorted to read Scripture (see Deut. 17:19; 31:11; Isa. 34:16; Neh. 8:18; Col. 4:16; I Thess. 5:27).

Reading the Bible gives us the "big picture" of what God is doing in the Word. It reveals His character, His thoughts, and His emotions. It lets us know what God thinks about certain things, and how we should react to them. Thus, reading the Bible is not only important, but imperative for every Christian.

The tragedy today is that many Christians deprive themselves of a tremendous blessing by neglecting such a simple enjoyment as reading the Bible. With our present-day emphasis on "in-depth" Bible study and memorizing random Scripture verses, we're in danger of losing sight of the "big picture," the "whole counsel of God," which, as we noted earlier, we discover when we read through the Bible regularly.

To help guide us in this regard, there are a number of through-the-Bible-in-a-year reading plans from which to choose, or we can create our own plan. The important thing is that we get busy reading God's Word.

Remember, when reading the Bible, do just that—read. Resist the urge to underline or circle words and verses, or to slow down and consider a passage or a verse at a time. Instead, concentrate on reading the passage with the flow in which it was written.

Bear in mind that there are various "genres" (kinds) of Biblical literature. There are the flowing narratives of the Old Testament, and the rhythmic beauty of the poetic books. There's the flaming oratory of the Old Testament prophets and their powerful "thus says the Lord" decrees to ancient Israel.

In stark simplicity, the Gospel accounts record the life and ministry of Jesus. There's the apocalyptic symbolism of Daniel and Revelation, and the wonderful didactic style of the New Testament letters. Read each of the various genres, taking note as you read of the historical setting, time frame, and sequencing of events, as well as the ramifications of those events.

Don't get sidetracked. This is reading time. Trying to work out the full meaning and interpretation of a passage is an activity for study time, which we'll cover in our next section.

Bible reading furnishes us with the necessary background information we need as we undertake subsequent study of the Scriptures. Indeed, the more familiar we become with the material in the Bible, the more we will get out of not only study, but subsequent meditation, memorization, and Bible teaching, as well.

Study

"Turning your ear to wisdom and applying your heart to understanding, and if you call out for insight and cry aloud for understanding, and if you look for it as for silver and search for it as for hidden treasure, then you will understand the fear of the Lord and find the knowledge of God." (Prov. 2:2-5)

> The heights by great men reached and kept
> Were not attained by sudden flight,
> But they, while their companions slept,
> Were toiling upward in the night.
>
> (Henry Wadsworth Longfellow)

Diligent, intense Bible study is the best way we can go about applying our heart to understanding. The treasures of God's Word are for those who will make

Bible study a priority, rearranging busy schedules in order to set aside quality hours for it.

How do we undertake a Bible study? Do we study the Bible in the same way we would a textbook at school? Are there any rules or guidelines we need to keep in mind as we study the Bible?

Guidelines for Bible Study

While the Bible may be God's textbook for living, this in no way implies that we should study it as we would any other textbook. The Bible is dynamic and alive. It is the revelation of God to man. Studying the Bible is not a mere academic exercise. We are not studying the Bible so we can know "all the facts" about God, we are studying the Bible in order that we might know God better. We want revelation and understanding of who God is and how He wants us to live and conduct our lives. You don't need to be a genius or an academic giant to study God's Word. Bible study is for every Christian. It's a life-building process that has nothing to do with I.Q. or grade-point averages.

As we enter into the study of God's Word, there are a number of accepted general rules to follow. Thus, laid out below are a number of things to keep in mind as we launch into Bible study.

The first thing we must do as we begin studying a passage of Scripture is to ask the right questions of the text.

Observation—What does the passage really say? This is discovered simply by reading the text, and thinking about what we have read. It is often a good idea to read the passage in several different translations of the Bible. The Bible was originally written in Hebrew, Chaldean, and Greek, so different translations of the Bible can shed light on different shades of meaning, and give us a better understanding of what the original writer was really saying.

Interpretation—What does the passage really mean? Interpretation is a word that seems to unnecessarily scare many Christians. But, though we may want to deny it, every time we read something, we interpret it.

I am involved in a missions organization which has people from hundreds of denominations in over one hundred countries. It becomes almost comical at times the way we seem to come up with such differing positions on an issue.

On some issues, we simply have to "agree to disagree" in love. If you were to ask each person in the mission if they have a "grid" or a preconceived idea through which they run the Bible as they read it (be it either denominational or personal taste), I'm quite certain they would all deny it. "What we have arrived at is the plain meaning of the text," they would proclaim.

We all too often have a number of different "plain meanings of the text" floating around at the same time! Thus, the question is not, "Do we interpret what we read?" but, "Are we interpreting it correctly?"

In my years as a Christian, I have seen enough shattered and burned-out Christian lives, resulting from wrong interpretations of the Bible, to know that there are accepted rules to follow in interpreting Scripture. When these rules are broken, confusion and spiritual shipwreck result. There are too many dead snake-handlers in the hills of Tennessee who claimed to have had the "right" interpretation of Mark 16:18. There have been too many tragic instances of diabetics dying because a certain interpretation of Scripture demanded they "walk by faith" and stop taking their insulin. Too many children have died because their parents withheld treatment or medication because of erroneous interpretations of Scripture. The ramifications of wrong interpretations of Scripture can be dire indeed, both physically and spiritually.

For more information on the principles of Bible interpretation, see Appendix I.

Application—What does the passage mean to me? All Bible study is pointless unless, after having discerned the meaning of a passage, we apply it to our lives. So, what is God saying to us through the particular portion of Scripture we are studying?

Some passages of Scripture are universally applicable to every Christian, such as "...love one another..." "...clothe yourselves with humility..." (John 13:34, I Pet. 5:5). Other verses are not so clear.

Should I really greet all the brethren with a holy kiss (I Thess. 5:26)? Do I really need to go to Troas to get Paul's cloak and take it to Rome (II Tim. 4:13)? Do I need to throw the little ones against the rocks in order to be happy (Ps. 137:9)? On a date with my wife, should I tell her that she reminds me of the horses in Pharaoh's chariots, or that her hair is like a flock of goats, and her neck is like a tower David built for an army (S. of Sol. 1:9; 4:1,4)? Thus, we must discern carefully not only the meaning and interpretation of a verse, but also its application for our life.

There are times when the Holy Spirit will speak a verse or passage to us for direct application to a situation we face, in much the same way as the Lord spoke Ephesians 5:26 to me on the beach in Santa Cruz. Studying for application, however, is more objective than this, yet every bit as personal.

For instance, my wife undertook a study on the responses of the disciples to persecution in the book of Acts. What she gleaned during this study, she was able to apply to her life in dealing with people who try to use intimidation to control her. Through careful study of Paul's activities in Thessalonica (Acts 17; I Thess. 1 and 2), I discovered ten principles of evangelism which have greatly helped me in winning people to Christ. (See "Paul's Principles of Evangelism," pages

37-73, *Bringin' 'Em Back Alive*, Danny Lehmann, Whitaker House, 1987.)

All the Bible study in the world will do us not one bit of good if we fail to apply it to our lives. The only way to measure effective Bible study is not by how much we know, but by its work in our lives.

Is Bible study producing fruit in your life? If not, reread the points listed above, and ask God to show you why it has not been the life-changing instrument He promised it would be.

There are many good books (see Appendix II) that give further details regarding Bible study. I trust, however, that I have awakened your appetite to dig deep for truth from God's Word, as though you were searching for hidden treasure—because you are!

A Word About Christian Books

While not a substitute for the Bible, reading Christian books can enhance our Bible study and greatly supplement our Christian growth. More than once, at a crucial time of need in my life, God has used a Christian book to speak a "word in season" (Isa. 50:4 KJV) to me.

Once, after the Holy Spirit had deeply convicted me of pride, the Lord spoke to my heart through *The Calvary Road*, by Roy Hession. At another time, when I needed faith for victorious living, the Lord was able to speak to me through *The Christian's Secret to a Happy Life*, by Hannah Whithall Smith, and set me free to trust Him.

I will forever bless the day that someone recommended the book *Ordering Your Private World*, by Gordon MacDonald. The message of this book has radically altered my life, and indirectly inspired me to write this book.

A practice I have found helpful in relation to Christian books is to read books on a number of different subjects. As an example, I tend to gravitate toward books that interest me because of my calling (books on evangelism, missions, discipleship, and leadership). However, I try to maintain a balance by reading books on other subjects, especially those related to character development (prayer, humility, holiness, suffering, and the like).

I also like to read and keep abreast of books that are selling well because of a particular message God seems to be saying to the Church, books such as *The Late Great Planet Earth*, by Hal Lindsay, which awakened the interest of the Church in Bible prophecy in the early 1970s, or Frank Peretti's two novels, *This Present Darkness* and *Piercing the Darkness*, which in the late 1980s and early 1990s has focused the attention of Christians on the victory that is ours in Jesus over the surrounding darkness of the present age. I have also found it helpful to read books from the different eras of church history.

There are those authors whose "specialty" lies in a particular area, such as James Dobson on the family, Josh McDowell on apologetics, or E.M. Bounds on prayer. I like to read present-day authors such as Swindoll, MacDonald, and Stanley, but I also like to read authors of a century ago, such as Charles Finney and William Booth. I also read Wesley and Whitefield, Christian authors of two centuries ago.

I read Luther, Calvin, and other leaders of the Reformation, and periodically, I read the writings of the Early Church fathers or church history books. I also enjoy the books of such Christian mystics as Thomas a Kempis and Madame Guyon, not to mention the timeless Christian classics such as *Pilgrim's Progress* or *In His Steps*, and classic Christian authors like Spurgeon, Tozer, and Murray.

I would suggest a regular discipline of book reading. I presently average reading two books each month. (One preacher I know reads six books a week!)

As with the other disciplines, seek the Lord, set your goals, establish your priorities, and practice the discipline of book reading.

The reward you receive in spiritual growth is well worth the price of setting aside lesser things to allow yourself time to read. George Verwer, Director of Operation Mobilisation, has put it well: "Readers make leaders."

Hearing

"He wakens...my ear to listen like one being taught." (Isa. 50:4)

"Garbage in, garbage out" is a phrase that has become popular in the computer age. It refers to the cause and effect relationship between the programming of information into a computer and what we can then expect to receive back from the computer. If the information going in is garbled, the information coming out will be garbled, as well.

The same is true with our minds. What we feed into our minds is ultimately what is going to come out. Most of the information that feeds into our minds is received either by seeing or hearing. We have already covered many of the "seeing" aspects in our discussion about reading and studying God's Word. Now it is time to look more closely at hearing as a way of storing God's Word in our heart.

The Bible has a lot to say about the things we allow into our minds through our ears. We're told not to listen to gossip and slander (Prov. 18:8; 20:19; 26:20; I Tim. 5:19), not to receive accusations against elders (I Tim. 5:19), not to listen to ungodly counsel (Ps. 1:1; Prov. 1:10), and in general, to listen to things that are spiritually edifying (Prov. 8:34; Luke 8:15; James 1:19; I Cor. 14).

Listed below are a number of helps that have helped me to increase my capacity to "hear" what God is saying to me through His Word.

Hearing Aids

1—Develop a hearing ear. "Ears that hear and eyes that see—the Lord has made them both" (Prov. 20:12.)

When, after telling the parable of the sower, Jesus exhorts, "He who has ears to hear, let him hear" (Mark 4:9), He is not referring to physical ears, but to an attitude of heart that is receptive and teachable. The Bible enjoins us to search for truth as for hidden treasure (Prov. 2:2-5), and calls those who "hunger and thirst for righteousness" blessed (Matt. 5:6).

The people Jesus is addressing are those whose desire for righteousness is so great that they sift His words to find the spiritual significance, as a person would sift sand in search of hidden treasure. Tragically, I have spoken with many Christians in my travels who have lost their hunger and thirst for righteousness and truth. They wander like spiritual deaf-mutes, totally oblivious to anything God may be wanting to say to them.

We must develop hearing ears. The first step in this process is learning to recognize the voice of the Lord. A newborn baby does not automatically recognize its mother's voice. But as time goes by, it learns to recognize that voice. Even in the midst of other voices and noises, it can recognize its mother.

In the same way, new babes in Christ must learn to recognize the voice of the Lord. At first, they may make mistakes in recognizing it, but as time goes by, they should be able to recognize His voice in the confusion of today's world. If we ask God to help us recognize His voice when He speaks, He will be faithful to help us. But, of course, the desire to hear God's voice is based on our desire for spiritual truth. If we have no desire for righteousness and truth, we have little need of recognizing God's voice, since it is full of righteousness and truth.

If we are bored with sermons, Bible studies, teaching tapes, and discussions about the Bible, there is a good chance that our spiritual ears have gone deaf. But, unlike physical deafness, spiritual deafness is a reversible ailment.

If we will humble ourselves before God, and admit our need and dependence upon Him, He will unstop our deafened ears. But we must make His word our priority. We must read His word, diligently study it, and attend meetings where His word is being taught. When we do this, we will begin to hear what the Spirit is saying to the Church (Rev. 3:22).

2—Learn to take notes. "...And what he wrote was upright and true" (Ecc. 12:10).

Someone has said, "the weakest ink is better than the strongest memory." Speech professors tell us that under normal circumstances, we remember only seven percent of what we hear. Hence, it becomes vitally important for us that we learn to take notes. College students listen to a lecture and take copious notes so they can review them later to better retain what was taught in the lecture. How much more should we be doing the same, in order to retain God's Word in our hearts?

The literal meaning of the word *disciple* is "learner" or "student," and that's exactly how we should approach the Word of God. Whether the Word is being preached or taught from the pulpit, or whether we are reading and studying it for ourselves, we should approach it with the same fervor as a college student pursuing a degree in their chosen field of endeavor.

Taking notes, especially when we attend meetings, reinforces that we are a disciple—a learner—and not merely a spectator. If God's Word is being taught, we should automatically assume that God may want to speak to us through what is said. Thus, a notebook should be the very next thing we pick up after our

Bible, as we head out to a meeting. It doesn't matter how boring the speaker may seem—God can still speak to us. God doesn't choose to speak only through dynamic and gifted speakers. He can and will speak through whomever He chooses—after all, he spoke to Balaam through a donkey (Num. 22:21-41)! We should always be attentive to hear what God may be saying to us, regardless of who is speaking.

I'm sure that those who have been through college can identify with this. Not every lecture given in the course of pursuing a degree is dynamic. In fact, many of them are boring and mundane. But the student needs to know and understand what the lecturer is speaking about—it is vital information for their chosen field of expertise. So they force themselves to listen and take notes. God wants to, and will, speak to us. The key is to be ready and listening. We can't allow our dissatisfaction with the delivery style of the messenger to distract us from the message.

My wife likes to keep separate notebooks for the various meetings she attends. She has one notebook for Sunday morning sermons and another for the various other teaching sessions she attends. I have a wide-margin Bible, and often like to print the notes right in the margin next to the passage being taught upon. I also have friends who have filled up notebooks with Scripture references and created their own personal "concordances." How we do it is not as important as the fact that we begin to do it. Note- taking is imperative in developing a hearing ear.

3—Use a cassette tape player. In my opinion (of course, I'm biased!), one of the greatest inventions in history is the cassette player, especially the "Walkman" type. Through the various denominations and ministries in our land, Christians have literally thousands of Bible teaching and preaching cassette tapes at their disposal. Many of these churches and organizations offer the tapes free through tape lending libraries. This is not counting the availability of a vast array of inexpensive recordings of the reading of Bible text.

A cassette player allows us to take advantage of this resource and fill in those "dead times" during the day, when our body may be physically engaged in doing something, but our mind is not. I manage, on average, to get about ten extra hours of spiritual "feeding" each week through the use of cassette teaching tapes. I listen to tapes as I do my morning stretches, while I'm out running, when I'm cleaning my office, shaving, taking a shower, and other bathroom activities. When I'm driving alone in my car, I listen to tapes or recite previously memorized Scripture.

At home in the evening, I like to wash the dishes. I must confess that I have mixed motives. Not only does it give my wife a break, but it provides me with about thirty minutes in which to enjoy some extra spiritual "feeding" with the help of my tape player.

Learn to take advantage of the technology we have at our disposal to redeem the time wisely and turn "dead times" into "live times" of spiritual feeding. All it takes is a little discipline.

Meditation

"Do not let this Book of the Law depart from your mouth; meditate on it day and night, so that you may be careful to do everything written in it. Then you will be prosperous and successful." (Josh. 1:8)

"The devotional practice of pondering the words of a verse, or verses of Scripture, with a receptive heart, allowing the Holy Spirit to take the written Word and apply it as the living Word to the inner being," is how Campbell McAlpine defines meditation. Of the five ways to hide God's Word in our heart, meditation is probably the most subjective, and could be seen as rather "mystical." Because of this, many Christians, especially those in Western society (which tends to major on logic and objectivity), miss out on the blessings of Bible meditation.

With the invasion of Eastern thought into our culture, anything that smacks of mysticism is dismissed as Eastern or New Age ideology. But it need not be. We must not allow counterfeits from Eastern and New Age thought to turn us off from the true practice of Bible meditation.

A look from Scripture at the benefits to those who practice Bible meditation ought to be enough to motivate us into it. If we look closely at Joshua 1:8, we see that not only are we promised prosperity and success if we meditate, but that meditation is linked with what we say ("Do not let this Book of the Law depart from your mouth...").

It is an interesting study to see the connection in the Bible between what is in our heart and what comes out of our mouth (See Rom. 10:9-10; Matt. 12:34-36; II Cor. 6:11; Ps. 45:1-2).

Meditation, therefore, will help us to bridle our tongue (James 3:3). David opened the Psalms by listing the benefits for those who meditate. Those who meditate, he tells us, will be blessed (Ps. 1:1). They will be nourished and refreshed: "He is like a tree planted by streams of water..." (Ps. 1:3). They will be productive: "...which yield its fruit in season..." (Ps. 1:3); persevering: "...whose leaf does not wither..." (Ps. 1:3); and successful: "...Whatever he does prospers" (Ps. 1:3). David also used words like *Maskil* (a meditative, contemplative poem) and *Selah* (a pause for reflection) in his psalms to get the reader to slow down and let the message "sink in."

Unfortunately, some erroneous New Age techniques have been allowed into the Church to "assist" us in the area of our meditation experience. Instructions to let our mind journey back to Palestine and "visualize" the sun reflecting off Jesus' hair, and smell the flowers in the field where He fed the five thousand, are dangerously close to occultic and esoteric practices.

True Bible meditation is not an esoteric practice. Bible meditation always has an object. We are instructed in Scripture to meditate upon God's character (Deut. 32:4; Ps. 145:17), God's creation (Ps. 19), God's Word (Ps. 1:1-2; 119:97; Josh. 1:8), and God's works (Ps. 77:11-12; 143:5).

The writer to the Hebrews tells us to "fix our eyes" on Jesus. The verb the writer uses here comes from a word early astronomers used to describe the way they gazed steadfastly at the stars. So in Bible meditation, we are fixing our eyes on firm, objective things.

The only meditation "technique" we need to practice in Bible meditation is the discipline to be still: "Be still, and know that I am God..." (Ps. 46:10). As we do this, we can ask the Holy Spirit to minister to us as we reflect upon individual verses and phrases from Scripture. Then, revelation from the Throne of heaven will flood our spirits with personal, intimate, and relevant truth, that will do nothing but help us fall more in love with the great God we serve.

God's Word, hidden in our hearts, is like the fuel that powers our spiritual life. As we draw on it, we are empowered, renewed, and refreshed by the Lord. If we are to live an effective Christian life, and claim our rightful prize at the end, then we need this fuel. We need God's Word hidden in our heart—and not just once. Like any fuel source, it must be continually replenished. We must develop a daily discipline of spending time reading, studying, meditating upon, and hearing the Word of God. If we want the prize, we can do no less.

Chapter Five

100 Trillion Bits is a Lot of Memory

Bible Memorization

"I have hidden your word in my heart that I
might not sin against you" (Ps. 119:11).

Sometimes when I'm preaching, I like to ask my
audience: "How many of you have tried a program of
Bible memorization and failed, and as a result gave
up?" Usually about seventy-five percent of the people
raise their hands.

Why is this so? Perhaps the biggest reason is the
spiritual warfare we encounter when we endeavor to
memorize God's Word and hide it in our hearts. Satan
is well aware of the benefits of Scripture memorization. He hates for us to hide God's Word in our heart
and, therefore, loves to condemn us with our failures.
He knows that the memorized Word of God is an
effective weapon against him as he seeks to entice us
to sin. Jesus demonstrated this point during His time
in the wilderness (Matt. 4; Luke 4).

Satan also wants to keep us ignorant of God's
promises, and thereby make it impossible for us to
appropriate them. Finally, he wants to keep us in
bondage both to sin and to subtle legalism, because he
knows all too well the words of Jesus, "...You will

know the truth, and the truth will set you free" (John 8:32). Our capacity to experience true freedom is increased as we make more truth available to our hearts. Hence, we need to memorize Scripture.

Scientists tell us that the human mind is capable of storing 100 trillion bits of information. For you non-computer experts, that's a lot of information! Surely we should be making a little effort to fill up at least some of those bits with God's Word.

Young Muslim men, I am told, must memorize the entire Koran (approximately as long as the New Testament) before they are allowed to enter the University of Cairo. Other people spend years memorizing information, just for a chance to win money on one of the many game shows that proliferate on American TV. How much more should we be motivated to hide God's Word in our hearts?

There are a number of memory techniques for use in memorizing Scripture. Jerry Lucas suggests imagining an odd-looking object and associating a Bible passage to the image in your mind. Others suggest taking a walk along a familiar street and "hanging" verses on the various landmarks along the street. Some say that writing verses out longhand is helpful.

In my own experience with Scripture memorization, I have discovered two principles and two practices which have helped me greatly. They are born out of both my successes and failures with memorization. In the remainder of this chapter, I will share these principles and practices with you.

Two Principles
Principle 1—You must love the Word. Remember English Literature in high school? The teacher could recite line after line of Shakespeare, or verse after verse of Milton. We wondered, "How on earth do they remember all that stuff?" They remembered all those lines because they loved them. For them, nothing was

of greater pleasure than to sit for hours and read Shakespeare and the poets, absorbing not only what was said, but how it was said.

The same is true for the Christian. It is highly unlikely that we will ever develop a consistent discipline of Bible memorization if we do not love God's Word. The Bible writers spoke often and passionately about their love affair with the Holy Scriptures. David set aside 176 verses of Psalm 119 to express his regard and love for the Scriptures.

If we don't have this kind of love for the Word of God, then we need to humbly ask the Lord to give us such a love for His word. It is a prayer God is delighted to answer. By His grace He will create in our hearts a hunger and thirst for righteousness and truth that can only be satisfied by spending time reading, studying, hearing, meditating upon, and memorizing His word.

Principle 2—Scripture memorization does not depend upon human I.Q. There is a distinction between our mind (intellectual capacity) and our human spirit (spiritual capacity). Paul told the intellectual Greeks at Corinth that God's truth was learned spiritually, not intellectually (I Cor. 2:9-16). Jesus said that it is the Holy Spirit who would bring His truth to our memory (John 14:26). Later, He taught His disciples not to think ahead of time about what they would say when under persecution, but that the Father would give them the words (Matt. 10:17-20). Our human spirit, in communion with God's Spirit, is like a "storage tank" for His word, and the capacity of our spirit has nothing to do with our I.Q.

Paul prayed the Ephesian Christians would have spiritual understanding. He exhorted them to be renewed in the *spirit* of their minds (Eph. 1:18; 4:24). This is not to say that our mind is evil or unimportant. Quite the opposite is true. We are to love God with all our mind (Matt. 22:37). We are merely recognizing the dynamic of God's Spirit working in our spirit to bringing us both revelation and remembrance of God's truth (Rom. 8:16).

I mentioned in the previous chapter how, shortly after my conversion, God gave me a promise that He would cleanse my mind from the effects of psychedelic drugs. Drugs had taken such a toll on my mind that I couldn't hold down a job which required a memory span longer than a few minutes. But as I made God's Word a priority in my life, He began stretching and restoring my memory span, and gave me the capacity to remember hundreds of Bible verses. Not only this, but I was able to work at jobs other than washing dishes, washing cars, or other assembly line work.

I recount my experience because it confirms what has been said. My I.Q. had nothing to do with what God did in my mind. It was a work of His Spirit. "...'Not by might nor by power, but by my Spirit,' says the Lord Almighty" (Zech. 4:6).

Ask the Holy Spirit to make this true in your life. Ask Him to fill your spirit with His word. As you believe, He will store up His word in your spirit.

Two Practices

Practice 1—Repetition. I have tried a number of memory techniques, and am convinced that for a consistent program of Bible memorization, there is no substitute for the simple discipline (there's that word again!) of repeating Scripture until it is lodged in our spirit.

Memorizing whole chapters and books of the Bible, rather than isolated verses, has been a great help to me. I am not opposed to memorizing individual verses (they are especially helpful in witnessing), but we must remember that the Bible is not a jigsaw puzzle where we choose the pieces we like. Actually, verses are a late addition to the Scripture text. The books of the Bible were originally written in continuous, flowing prose, broken up into paragraphs, not verses. Thus, reading chapters and books, memorizing them as an integrated whole, and not as isolated verses, enhances our understanding of Scripture.

How do you start memorizing Scripture? Let me demonstrate. I memorized I Peter. I started at the beginning: "Peter, an apostle of Jesus Christ, To God's elect, strangers in the world, scattered throughout Pontus, Galatia, Cappadocia, Asia and Bithynia." I repeated this phrase over and over until I could say it without looking at the page. Then I moved on to the next phrase: "who have been chosen according to the foreknowledge of God the Father, through the sanctifying work of the Spirit...." Again, I repeated this phrase until I could quote it without looking at the page.

Then I strung all the phrases I had learned together, and recited verses, paragraphs, and chapters, until I was able to recite the whole book. This may seem tedious, but it's really not. It's like a snowball tumbling down a snow-covered hill; once you start, your collection of memorized Scripture, and your love for the process of memorizing it, will keep growing.

I would suggest you start in the following way. Start by learning your favorite Bible chapter (Ps. 23; I Cor. 13; John 3; Rom. 8). The fact that it is your favorite chapter gives you a head start in memorizing it. I would suggest avoiding Psalm 119 or anything in Leviticus as your favorite chapter (for obvious reasons), at least until you get started!

At your most alert time of the day, set aside thirty minutes to recite your favorite chapter from the translation of the Bible you like the best. You'll be amazed at how much of the chapter you've already committed to memory. Build on what you already know, and if need be, fill in any memory gaps. Continue to repeat the half hour each day, until you have the whole chapter memorized. You'll be amazed at what memorizing your first chapter does for your confidence.

Once you have your first chapter down pat, you can begin adding new ones, as the Lord leads. If you follow this pattern, you will soon have a vast repertoire of Scripture committed to memory. From this repertoire, God can quicken verses and passages to your heart and mind, and speak to you through them. This is not to mention the inestimable value these Scriptures will be as you share the Gospel with others.

I would encourage you, however, that whatever memory system you decide to use, use it consistently. After your initial chapter is memorized, you might like to proceed to a small New Testament book such as Titus, II Peter, James, or I John. You may not always be able to commit a half hour each day to memorization. But I think it's better to try for five minutes of Scripture memorization each day, rather than 30 minutes once a week. Scripture memorization needs to become a habitual process in our life, and habits are more strongly and quickly build by repeating something daily. Once we have this practice down, we are ready to implement the next one.

Practice 2—Review. After we have committed a number of Scriptures to memory, we need to make sure they stay there. This means we must make a regular commitment to review the Scriptures we have learned.

A temptation to avoid when memorizing Scripture is to add too many Scriptures too quickly. The aim of memorizing, after all, is so that we can recall from our memory the Scriptures we have learned. If we are flooding our memory with so many new Scriptures that it loses track of the old ones we've learned, then we are defeating our purpose. Thus, we must review what we have learned on a regular basis, so we don't lose track of it.

I have found it helpful to use a portion of my morning Quiet Time for committing new Scriptures to memory, reserving my review time for some of those "dead times" we talked about under "Hearing" in the previous chapter.

For instance, I had to drop my two boys off at school this morning. After dropping them off, it takes me about 15-20 minutes in traffic to get home, so I used this time for review. On the drive home, I was able to go over in my mind and recite out loud six chapters from the book of Romans. Not only was I spiritually edified by redeeming the time in this way, but I kept myself from the temptation to complain about the traffic, listen to people pool their ignorance on radio talk shows, or just daydream the time away.

Since I run alone a lot to keep in shape for the marathon, I find this a good time for reviewing Scripture. I'll often play games with myself to make it fun. For example, on an identical five-mile run, I might recite six chapters on Tuesday, then on Wednesday, I'll set out to break my record by trying to recite seven or eight chapters.

You could do the same when driving long distances, or when walking between appointments or errands. Occasionally, when I am tempted to get angry and "pop off" at someone or something, I recite a chapter to myself.

Shopping is not one of my favorite activities. But since my wife enjoys it so much, I choose to try and enjoy it with her. The emphasis was always on the "try," until I discovered that while my wife was taking her time meandering through a store, I could follow along, slowly reciting Scriptures to myself. Shopping, for me, has gone from drudgery to a time of recharging my spiritual batteries. What was once a cold, dry choice to "get into it" for my wife's sake has actually become fun!

Those who take the time to memorize Scripture will reap the benefit of their labor. They store within themselves a reservoir of divine inspiration from which they can draw as they resist temptation (Ps. 119:11; Luke 4:1-13). It is a reservoir that will also enhance their prayer life (Acts 4:24-28). It will aid them as they share the Gospel with non-Christians (Acts 2:16-36; 3:18; 17:2), and be an effective tool for redeeming otherwise wasted time (Eph. 5:16). Last, but certainly not the least, it will cause them to love the Lord more, and stand firm with Him in the face of any adversity Satan may bring.

Most of us, whether we realize it or not, are already on the path to Scripture memorization. If I were to ask you to recite John 3:16, you would almost automatically begin, "For God so loved the world..." and on you would go to recite the whole verse. You know it, because you love and believe the verse. You have read it time and again, and as a result, stored it away in your memory bank, where from time to time you review it.

The rest of the Bible is as simple to remember as John 3:16 was. The ball is in your court—all it takes is a little commitment and *discipline*!

Chapter Six

Fast Food

"Then John's disciples came and asked him,
'How is it that we and the Pharisees fast, but
your disciples do not fast?' Jesus answered,
'How can the guests of the bridegroom mourn
while he is with them? The time will come
when the bridegroom will be taken from them;
then they will fast '" (Matt. 9:14-15).

Perhaps more than any of the other disciplines discussed in this book, fasting brings to mind the idea of "discipline." It takes plain, old-fashioned, raw discipline to abstain from eating and drinking in order to give ourselves over to prayer. In none of the other disciplines does the flesh raise up its ugly head and demand its way as much as it does in the area of fasting.

The most cursory flip through the pages of the Bible quickly reveals the importance of fasting, and its benefits to our spiritual lives. Jesus, Paul, Hannah, Jonathan, David, Uriah, Anna, Esther, and many others included fasting as part of their devotional life to add intensity to their prayers.

During His temptation, as He was about to launch into ministry, Jesus used fasting as a weapon against Satan (Matt. 4:1-11). Fasting seemed to increase Jesus' spiritual power. The Bible records Jesus embarking upon His forty-day sojourn in the wilderness "full of the Spirit," and returning after the fast in the "power of the Spirit" (Luke 4:1-14).

Fasting was also common among such Old Testament leaders as Moses, David, Ezra, and Nehemiah (Ex. 34:28; II Sam. 3:35; Ezra 8:21-23; Neh. 1:7). Elijah, the prophet, fasted regularly (I Kings 19:8), as did Paul and the apostles in the New Testament (II Cor. 11:27). The Old Testament also records times of corporate fasting being proclaimed in the face of a national crisis (II Chr. 20:3; Est. 4:3; Jonah 3:5-9), and fasting being practiced by individuals who desperately needed to hear from God (I Sam. 1:7-8; II Sam. 12:16-23).

Fasting was also employed by the Early Church when they sent out missionaries (Acts 13:1-3), ordained elders (Acts 14:23), and as an essential part of apostolic ministry (II Cor. 6:5). Fasting was also an integral part of the lifestyle of saints such as Luther, Calvin, Knox, Wesley, Edwards, Finney, and other "movers and shakers" throughout church history.

The fifty-eighth chapter of the book of Isaiah gives us greater insight into the subject of fasting than any other chapter in the Bible. Isaiah begins with a warning about fasts which are unacceptable because of selfish motives (verses 3-5), and then goes on to list the purposes and benefits of fasting. The promises to those who fast God's way are health, answered prayer, guidance, fruitfulness, restoration, refreshment, and an impartation of God's righteousness and glory (verses 8-12).

In other places in the Bible, we are told that fasting humbles us (Ps. 35:13), and in a very real way, intensifies our prayer life (Ps. 35:13; 69:10). C.H. Spurgeon said: "Our seasons of fastings and prayer at the Tabernacle have been high days indeed; never has heaven's gate stood wider; never have our hearts been nearer the central glory."

In light of this biblical and historical evidence, it seems that fasting has never been an optional extra for Christians. Rather, it is an essential facet of discipleship.

From Feasting To Fasting

If fasting has not become a regular part of your spiritual discipline (between dinner and breakfast doesn't count!), then I would encourage you to follow the steps below as practical guides for entering into prayer and fasting.

1—Begin with a "partial" fast (Dan. 10:3). As with all of the disciplines discussed in this book, we must start out slow and build on our successes. For fasting, a partial fast is a good way to begin this process. A partial fast consists of restricting our diet to certain things. Thus, we may choose to eat no meat, or eat only fruit and vegetables. I would suggest a good place to start is a partial fast, where you restrict your diet to fruit and/or vegetable juices. Not only is this healthy, but it gives your mind and body a chance to get accustomed to feeling deprived.

2—Undertake a twenty-four hour "normal" fast. Fasting is normally for the duration of a day (Isa. 58:3-5), and consists of no food or drink, except water.

Be sure to consume plenty of water on a fast. This is not only important to flush your kidneys, but to prevent dehydration and sickness. Many Muslims have died while fasting in hot climates during their annual Ramadan fast in which for a month, they observe a total fast from sunrise to sunset. The body can go weeks without food, but can die in a few days without water.

A normal fast usually goes from breakfast to breakfast, and means missing two meals—lunch and dinner. Like the partial fast, a twenty-four hour normal fast provides you with the opportunity to experience, without being too much of a burden, the hunger pains and a little of the physical weakness that fasting produces. This will help as you prepare yourself physically and psychologically for longer fasts.

3—Pray often while fasting. The Bible emphasizes fasting with prayer. Thus, it is a good practice to set aside at least our normal meal times for prayer. By fasting, we also save the time normally spent in shopping for and preparing food. It is good to combine this time with the time we save by not eating, and spend it in unhurried prayer. There are times, of course, when we have to work or fulfill family duties. In these instances, God will give grace. As much as is possible, however, we should reserve fasting for times of solitude and prayer.

4—Fast consistently. It is a good idea to incorporate fasting into your regular devotional routine. Many Christians seem to wait for a crisis before they undertake a fast. But since their mind and body is not conditioned for fasting, they find it difficult to concentrate and pray about the crisis at hand. Instead of focusing on the crisis, they have visions of T-bone steaks and banana splits when they close their eyes to pray!

The Didache ("The Teaching of the Lord to the Twelve Apostles to the Gentiles") is a highly respected document dating from 70 to 110 A.D., which contains the teaching and practices of the Early Church. It taught that fasting should be practiced twice a week, on Wednesdays and Fridays.

John Wesley learned this, and made it mandatory for all of his early Methodist ministers to do the same, refusing to ordain any who didn't do it! Of course, we are under no obligation to fast twice a week, but nonetheless, regular fasting, as led by the Holy Spirit, is nothing but beneficial to our walk with the Lord.

I presently try to set aside each Monday for prayer and fasting, and, even though I need to work, I at least spend the breakfast and lunch hours with the Lord. I am even beginning to find that my stomach is getting used to fasting, and it is becoming less of a hardship.

There doesn't seem to be any biblical evidence that the more pain and discomfort you feel on a fast, the more "points" you score with God. The issue is that you are obeying Him and praying with fasting, not the decibel level of your groaning stomach!

There is also a fast I undertake once a month (on the first Friday of every month) in conjunction with Intercessors for America. The purpose of this fast is to pray for revival in my nation, but I have broadened the focus to include the particular nation in which I find myself on that Friday.

The Lord may direct you to regularly undertake a partial fast, such as giving up meat for one week a month, or fasting dinner once a week. Or, He may direct you to practice twenty-four hour fasts on a regular basis. In all of this, don't become legalistic, just be obedient, and the benefits of fasting mentioned in Isaiah 58 will be yours.

5—Undertake extended fasts. It is good periodically to set aside an extended amount of time for fasting and prayer. Times when we're facing a major decision—or experiencing an abnormally intense spiritual attack from the enemy—are usually good to undertake extended fasts. But again, the optimum is to undertake these extended times of fasting without a looming crisis.

Any fast that lasts longer than twenty-four hours is considered an extended fast. The Bible records people undertaking fasts for one, three, seven, ten, twenty-one, and forty days. I'm sure anything in between is quite acceptable to the Lord!

Surprisingly, fasts that last between one and three days are often the most difficult. This is because during the first three days of a fast, our body is busy cleansing itself of the toxic poisons that have built up in our system. After three days, most of the hunger pangs and headaches begin to go away, and our body enters a "cruise" phase that lasts well into the fast.

My experience tells me that sometimes this cruise phase is easier than other times. Some of my extended fasts have been more difficult than others. Each individual is different. But in general, the first three days are by far the hardest.

Somewhere between twenty-one and forty days, the hunger returns. This point is where starvation can set in, so it is advisable to begin eating again at this time.

When undertaking an extended fast, be ready to experience the most radical temptations to eat you'll ever experience! For some reason (not necessarily the devil!), the aroma of culinary delights continually seems to finds its way under our nostrils and beckons: "eat me!" During periods of extended fasting, I seem to get invited to more banquets and potluck dinners than at any other time. So, be forewarned—there will be temptations to eat, and eat big!

6—Participate in corporate fasts. Biblical leaders would often call times of corporate fasting. The Bible records an army (II Chr. 20:3), a city (Jonah 3:5-9), a group of leaders (Acts 13:1-3), and a whole nation (Lev. 16:29-31) fasting together as an expression of their solidarity and desire to seek God.

I know of one church that undertakes an annual three-day "fasting retreat," which centers around seeking God's blessing on the church and its members throughout the coming year. Not only does such a time provide a great opportunity for fellowship and spiritual refreshment, but, without the hassle of preparing and eating food, so much more time can be given to prayer and the Word. Another church I know of annually undertakes a three-week "Daniel fast," during which the members of the church eat only vegetables and drink water. Throughout the three weeks, much time is devoted to prayer.

Corporate fasting, like corporate prayer (Matt. 18:19), yields powerful results. Wise is the group that determines to undertake corporate fasting as part of their worship to the Lord.

7—Watch your motives. Jesus warns us very clearly about avoiding the temptation to let others know about our fasting as a way of showing how spiritual we are (Matt. 6:16-18). The Pharisees, it is said, would fast on Mondays and Thursdays, because they were market days, and more people would be around to admire their outward show of holiness and spirituality.

Jesus rebuked the Pharisees for their sham, and He will also rebuke us, if our motive for undertaking a fast is no more than wanting to inflate our ego and pride. We must be wary not to follow the example of the Pharisees (see also Isa. 58:3-5).

Of course, on an extended fast, we will lose weight (about a pound a day), and if people ask us how we're losing it, we must be honest with them. At the same time, we must guard against the subtle temptation to look unnecessarily gaunt and deprived, so that others will notice our piety. Alas, in such instances, pride— not piety—has become our motivation.

The physical ramifications of fasting are felt quicker than those of any of the other disciplines discussed in this book. Our belly throbs with pangs of hunger. Our appetite screams out to be satisfied. Our head aches, and our body feels weak. When we close our eyes, visions of food dance behind our eyelids, tempting us to reach out and eat. Even foods we don't like suddenly take on an enticing appeal, when seen through the eyes of hunger. Yet, despite the physical hardship, fasting is worthwhile and important for every Christian.

Throughout His sojourn on earth, Jesus devoted periods of His time to fasting. It was a priority for Him, and He would often withdraw into the wilderness for times of fasting and prayer. His disciples followed His example.

If the very Son of God found it necessary to spend time fasting and praying, how much more should we be following His example?

Chapter Seven

Solitary Confinement

"...and [Jesus] departed into a solitary place,
and there prayed" (Mark 1:35 KJV).

An acquaintance of mine, Richard Wurmbrand,
spent fourteen years of his life in a communist prison
camp in Rumania, because of his faith in Christ. Three
of those years were spent in solitary confinement,
where he slept with rats, sat in his own waste, and did
not see another color except the brown of his cell walls
and the grey of his prison clothes. In his book, *With God
in Solitary Confinement*, he describes the nearness of the
presence of God he felt during that time:

> Out of fourteen years under the Communists
> in Rumania, I spent three years alone in a cell
> thirty feet below ground, never seeing sun,
> moon or stars, flowers or snow, never seeing
> another man except for the guards and inter-
> rogators who beat and tortured me.

> I seldom heard a noise in that prison....I had
> no Bible, nor any other book....During that
> time I rarely slept at night. I slept in the
> daytime. Every night I passed the hours in
> spiritual exercises and prayer....

> There were times when I looked at the cup
> of water which I had in my cell to convince
> myself that I was not yet in hell....But even in

the moments of utter doubt and utter despair, we were not left to ourselves entirely. The one who promised "I am with you always" (in Hebrew he could say only *bekol iom*, which means literally translated, "every day the whole day") has proved to be faithful. So we were able to overcome.

In solitude, Richard Wurmbrand suffered the most humiliating circumstances, yet his testimony is not one of despair, but one of hope and strength. Indeed, in what humanly should have been his weakest moment, he was able to draw strength as he became conscious of the tangible nearness of God.

Jesus was well aware of this when He entered the wilderness to pray and fast before commencing His earthly ministry. The solitude of the desert was for Him a place of spiritual upbuilding and strength. Dallas Willard puts it this way in his book, *The Spirit of the Disciplines:*

> Most to whom I have spoken about this matter [solitude] are shocked at the suggestion that the "wilderness," the place of solitude and deprivation, was actually *the place of strength and strengthening* for our Lord and that the Spirit led him there—as he would lead *us* there—to ensure that Christ was in the best possible condition for the trial.
>
> In that desert solitude, Jesus fasted for more than a month. *Then*, and not before, Satan was allowed to approach him with his glittering proposals of bread, notoriety and power. Only then was Jesus at the height of his strength. The desert was his fortress, his place of power.

If solitude with God in the desert was the place of Jesus' power, then how much more do we today need that place of power? Alas, in the active society in which we live, words such as *silence* and *solitude* have little place in our vocabulary. Yet we all need solitude at some point in our lives. Psychologists recognize this among the dwellers of today's busy and crowded cities.

Have you ever ridden on the subway in a busy city and watched the people? Most often they seem sullen and somber, almost like robots. As they ride along, some retreat from those around them by reading the newspaper. Others read books, while others stare blankly out the window. Psychologists refer to this as "sensory overload." Being in an intense environment, where the senses are continually bombarded from all sides, pushes people to a point of "overload." Their natural reaction is to retreat into themselves and allow the solitude of that time to restore their overloaded senses.

Christians are not immune from this overload, and like everyone else, our senses are daily bombarded. But as Christians, we are also susceptible to what I call "spiritual sensory overload." We are barraged daily by spiritual forces that seek to accuse, confuse, deceive, terrify, and otherwise harass us. Even for the most spiritual among us, there is only so much one can take. Hence the need to draw strength through times of solitude and silence with the Lord.

Solomon declares in Ecclesiastes, "...Go near to listen rather than to offer the sacrifice of fools..." (Ecc. 5:1) and David longs in the Psalms, "...Oh, that I had the wings of a dove! I would fly away and be at rest—I would flee far away and stay in the desert; I would hurry to my place of shelter, far from the tempest and storm" (Ps. 55:6-8). These men knew how imperative it was to spend time alone with God. This time was the secret to their spiritual strength, and Scripture records the many great things each of them was able to accomplish in his lifetime. In the middle of our busy and stressful lives, we need to find the time to spend in solitude with God.

Jesus often broke away from His busy schedule in order to be alone. Instead of relying on human wisdom when choosing the twelve apostles, He "...went out to a mountainside to pray, and spent the night praying to God" (Luke 6:12). Rather than giving in to anger over the murder of His cousin, John the Baptist, He "...withdrew by boat privately to a solitary place..." (Matt. 14:13). When Jesus was tempted to be proud after times of successful ministry and the acclaim of the crowds, "Very early in the morning, while it was still dark, Jesus got up, left the house and went off to a solitary place, where he prayed" (Mark 1:35; 6:46; Luke 6:12).

There were also times when, for no apparent reason other than fellowship with His Father, the disciples would find Jesus alone, praying (Luke 11:1). Solitary time alone with His Father was a priority for Jesus. He would not allow the success of His ministry or the milling crowds that demanded that He minister to them divert Him from the source of His strength.

In our media-driven world, we have lost sight of this truth. Image, rather than substance, has become the all-important concern. This also is true of the Church. The gospel singer singing to thousands, the pastor behind the pulpit, and the television evangelist have become the focus of our attention. They, and not the man in the closet on his knees, have far too often become the symbols of our success. But real spiritual strength does not come from being "at the front," leading. Rather, it comes through spending time alone with God. Jesus never lost sight of this.

I am, by nature, fairly hyperactive. I have always found it difficult to get away by myself, sit down, shut up, and listen to God. Several years ago, as I sought God about this tendency, He led me to a prayer in

Jeremiah, "Oh, that I had in the desert a lodging place for travelers, so that I might leave my people and go away from them..." (Jer. 9:2).

I asked the Lord to give me such a place, and in that place, and every place since then where I have prayed that prayer, without exception, God has provided friends with "lodging places" that I could get away to for times of solitary fellowship with Him. Through this, God has shown me that He will "bend over backward" to help me find a place of solitude, if only I have the desire to be with Him.

Given the busyness of my schedule, I have found it helpful to schedule days of solitude into my planner, four months in advance. I look forward to these times with the Lord. I like to think of them as my "spiritual EKG"—an electrocardiogram, or heart test. Usually, I go to a friend's house in the country, while he and his wife are at work. I take along my Bible, prayer diary, and journal. I resist the temptation to prepare sermon notes or write an article, and silence my heart to listen. I ask questions of myself regarding my motives for doing what I do in the ministry. I examine my victories and my defeats over the previous four months, and ask God for insight into how I can practically apply the things He is teaching me to my life and character.

Human beings were created by God to be social creatures. We were made to interact and depend upon others, so it requires discipline to withdraw ourselves from all human relationships and spend extended time alone with the Lord. But the practical benefits far outweigh the needed discipline. Withdrawing from others for a time removes any props that others may be to us, and allows us to see ourselves as we really are.

"Solitary confinement" is a well-established practice in our prison systems. It is used to break down a prisoner's will by isolating him from other human beings. This isolation leads to alienation, and the

prisoner's will begins to crack. For the Christian, solitude is wholly different. We have willingly isolated
ourselves from other people, but we are not alone. God
is always there with us, and indeed, His presence
seems more real, since we are separated from the busyness of our relationships to other people.

Ultimately, it is faith in the biblical principles of
strength through weakness that will motivate us to
schedule and observe days of solitude. It is our statement of faith to the Lord that we trust Him, and not
our work, our friends, or our circumstances to sustain
our life, ministry, and joy (Ps. 16:11).

A Day of Solitude—Some Practical Helps

As with the other disciplines discussed in this
book, I suggest starting out with the little you can do,
then building upon it. If you have never spent an
extended amount of time doing nothing but waiting
upon and seeking God, then set a realistic goal and
follow it through. You could start by scheduling a
Saturday morning to go to a solitary place and be with
the Lord. The length of time or the frequency is not the
crucial thing, but rather, that you actually get started.
We should never despise the day of small beginnings
(Zech. 4:10).

I started my habit of solitude by setting aside one
day a year (usually during the first or second week of
January). This time turned out to be such a blessing to
my soul that I began scheduling more days of solitude.
At present, I set aside three days a year, one every four
months, as days of solitary confinement with the Lord.
I like to refer to them as "a day in the desert." I find
three days a year is consistent with the Old Testament
pattern: "Three times a year all your men are to appear
before the Sovereign Lord, the God of Israel" (Ex.
34:23). Today, solitary times with the Lord are an indis-
pensable part of my spiritual devotion to God.

During a day in the desert, I spend time taking prayer walks, having unhurried times of Bible meditation, and spending time in healthy introspection, assessing my spiritual growth. I spend time thanking the Lord for changes He has worked in my life, and I ask Him to be strong in my areas of weakness. At day's end, I am ready to return to my normal schedule, having God's objectives, goals, and priorities for my life for the time ahead.

As with my daily Quiet Times, I have five main areas on which I concentrate for goal setting. They are: personal character development, family, ministry, leadership, and personal evangelism. I evaluate my success or failure at reaching my goals. If I have succeeded in reaching those goals, I set new ones. If I have failed in reaching a goal, I ask the Lord for understanding. Was it a realistic goal? Was I disobedient? Did I allow other things to crowd out the importance of attaining that goal?

When I have some understanding as to why I failed to attain the goal, I may reestablish it as my goal in that area. I may modify it to make it more realistic and attainable. Such goals are both spiritual and practical. For example, I may set a goal to run in a marathon, or hike up a mountain that I've never climbed. It might be to read through the Bible in a certain amount of time, or memorize the book of James.

I may decide to fast once a month, or read one Christian book each month. I find it helpful to set spiritual, physical, and practical goals, as well. What is important is that the goals develop me physically, mentally, emotionally, and spiritually, so that I can serve the Lord better in each of the five categories I mentioned.

So, for example, under "family," I might set goals such as a weekly Tuesday night date with my wife, nightly devotions with my boys, or a family vacation.

Under "ministry," I may set a goal to write a book, teach a weekly Sunday School class, or feed the homeless once a week. Under "leadership," I may ask God to help me train three evangelists, pioneer a new ministry, or write a monthly newsletter to those under my leadership. Under "personal evangelism," I may set a goal to win a certain amount of people to Christ, write a gospel tract for my personal use, or personally disciple two people.

A day of solitude is not just a day of inactivity where you vegetate before the Lord, but it's a day full of active fellowship with God, both reflecting on the past and preparing for the future.

As was mentioned earlier in our discussion on fasting, you don't need a crisis to develop before you take the time to get away with God in a time of solitude. Some of my most blessed times of solitude with the Lord have been when nothing special has been on my mind. Unshackled from any other worries, I was totally free to spend my time ministering to the Lord (Acts 13:1-3) and allowing Him, in turn, to bless me with His presence.

Below are some helpful practices for an effective day of solitude. But remember, they are general guidelines, not laws.

1—Where to go. Find a physical place where you can be away from people, telephones, and interruptions. Perhaps you know someone who lives in the country who would let you use their house while they are away at work. If the weather permits, you could go to a forest, a beach, or up to the mountains. If all else fails, you can rent a motel room. The cost is worth the time alone with the Lord.

2—Things to bring. From experience, I have found it best to limit myself to taking my Bible, prayer diary, and journal along with me. Solomon said there is a time for everything (Ecc. 3:1), and a day of solitude is a time for slowing down to reflect and listen to the Lord. Thus, books, magazines, or newspapers tend to distract me from doing just that. On more than one occasion, when using a friend's house as a place of solitary refuge, I have wasted hours thumbing through their bookshelf or tape collection, and been frustrated at the end of the day when I did not reach my objective.

3—What to do. Under normal circumstances, it is a good idea to fast during your day of solitude, not only for the spiritual benefits, but also for the time you save by not having to prepare and eat meals. In a sense, during a day of solitude, you are fasting from people, television, video, radio, and all other distractions, so why not food as well?

For me, a typical day of solitude runs as follows: when I arrive at my destination, I spend fifteen to thirty minutes doing nothing except quieting my heart before the Lord: "Be still and know that I am God" (Ps. 46:10). Such a period of time gives my mind and body a chance to adjust to the cessation of activity to which it is accustomed.

Then I may take a slow, relaxed, contemplative prayer walk. This is not a time of fervent intercession, but simply a time to enjoy God and His creation. This is why going to a forest, deserted beach, or to the mountains, away from man-made things, is a good idea, when possible.

If there are specific things which God wants to speak to me during this time, I jot them down in my journal or prayer diary. After a prayer walk, I spend time in "healthy introspection," assessing how well I've done in my spiritual life since my last time of solitude. "Examine yourselves to see whether you are in the faith; test yourselves" (II Cor. 13:5).

There is a kind of introspection which can be damaging, when we try to get so deep into our psyche that we begin to condemn ourselves, or find things that aren't really there. This is why an excessive digging into our past or present can be harmful. Healthy introspection simply evaluates our spiritual condition and the degree of our success or failure at walking in the faith.

After a time of introspection, I identify areas of my life that I feel need work, and begin to pray accordingly. If there has been any correction brought to me by other people, or by the Lord, I pray about it. I pray fervently for changes in areas of my character where change is needed.

Following prayer, I like to spend an extended time reading and meditating upon Scripture. On one occasion, I spent four hours reading twenty-five chapters of Isaiah, making notations in the margin of my Bible as I went along. At other times, the Holy Spirit has directed me to meditate upon one of Paul's missionary journeys, one of the pastoral epistles, or even single verses of Scripture.

During one of these times of meditation, I received a "life verse" from the Lord. I have spoken with others who also have felt a particular verse of Scripture characterized their life. With me, it was Isaiah 55:4, which speaks of the main areas to which God has called me: evangelism, leadership, and public speaking.

This provides a grid with which I can evaluate guidance and decision-making, according to the priorities God has given me. It also helps me see at a glance if any given activity in which I find myself involved is really in God's will ("...make your calling and election sure..." (II Peter 1:10).

Other times, I have received new sermons or a topical message that I feel impressed of the Lord to preach. Usually, though, I find the spiritual nourishment I receive during these times is more often directed at my own soul rather than others. Preachers need to be especially wary of always studying the Bible for the benefit of others, and not themselves.

Ultimately, where you go, what you bring, and what you do (and in what sequence) is yours to decide. As with all of the spiritual disciplines, though, to be truly spiritual, they must be led by the Holy Spirit and be free from legalism. We must practice freedom within the form. The mechanics change from time to time, depending upon the circumstances, but the intent and purpose remains the same.

If we will discipline ourselves to take solitary time alone with the Lord, we will not only reap the benefits already discussed in this chapter, but we will reap the supreme benefit: bringing joy to the heart of our heavenly Father, who delights to be in our presence more than we delight to be in His. It is there, in His presence, that there is "fullness of joy" (Ps. 16:11), both for ourselves and for God. It is a slice of heaven on earth.

Chapter Eight

Gimme a Break!

A few years ago, I was teaching at a Youth With A Mission Discipleship Training School in Kona, Hawaii. No sooner had I begun my message when my words began to slur, as though I were drunk. I felt dizzy, and began stumbling around in front of the class, finally knocking over the blackboard. I was forced to dismiss the class early and return to my room.

A doctor friend later examined me and told me that I was suffering from physical exhaustion. He suggested that I cancel my next week's schedule and spend the time just resting. I did, and shortly thereafter, I was physically restored.

I didn't need a brain surgeon to tell me why I was exhausted. I was responsible for a missionary training center with over 50 staff members, was trying to meet the deadline on a book I was writing, had a daily radio show, was constantly traveling, and had been training for a marathon race.

In addition, I had a wife (who had just had a baby by caesarean section), two boys, and an emotionally unstable tomcat! They all needed my attention. Then, to top it all off, I'd decided to go on an extended fast a few days before my trip to Kona. It all caught up with me in the front of the classroom in Kona. I was burned out!

As I rested the next week, I spent much time reflecting on my condition. I heard the Lord begin to speak to my heart about the need to take a sabbath. I began to see that in my zeal to avoid legalism, I had totally disregarded not only the law of God, but the *principle* of keeping the sabbath holy. My understanding of the sabbath grew as I undertook a Bible study on the subject and read the books *Ordering Your Private World* and *Restoring Your Spiritual Passion*, by Gordon MacDonald.

I am still convinced that we are under no legal obligation to keep the literal seventh day as a sabbath, but I am equally convinced that regardless of the day, "The sabbath was made for man..." (Mark 2:27), and we should take full advantage of anything God has made for us.

The word *sabbath* means "rest." God has created us in such a way that our minds and bodies need rest in order to stay healthy and productive. We have been programmed by God to conform to a cycle of work followed by rest. He created the day for men to work, and the night for them to rest. As well as this, He has commanded man to rest one day in seven (Ex. 23:12).

He demonstrated this principle by taking a day to rest after working the six days of creation (Gen. 2:2). Did God need a break? No, of course not. But knowing the intricate way He had created man, He chose to model for us the work/rest cycle by which we need to live. While God did not need to rest, nonetheless, Scripture declares that God refreshed Himself by observing the sabbath (Ex. 31:17).

Despite our theology of salvation by grace alone, those of us in the West are particularly prone to regard spirituality in terms of pleasing God through work accomplished. One entrepreneur told me, "Before I was saved, I worked sixty hours a week serving myself. I should work at least that much serving God."

But this type of drive is often motivated by the same fleshly motivations that, prior to conversion, motivated us in our worldly pursuits. All we have done is to dress them in spiritual clothes so they look "sanctified" in our eyes.

However, instead of being driven to complete work for God, we need to have our eyes opened to the necessity of building sabbath rest into our lives and schedules. Not only is this practice beneficial, but if we don't observe it, we are being disobedient to God, despite all our work and achievements. The Holy Spirit does not and will not drive or push us. Instead, He leads us, and one of the fruits of His leading is the ability to rest (Matt. 11:28).

The following are some markers to guide us in serving the Lord, while at the same time enjoying the rest we need in order to serve Him.

Steps to Sabbath Rest
1—Recognize the *principle* of sabbath rest. "Come to me, all you who are weary and burdened, and I will give you rest. Take my yoke upon you and learn from me, for I am gentle and humble in heart, and you will find rest for your souls" (Matt. 11:28-29).

We must view sabbath rest from God's perspective; it is a principle to be applied, not a legal standard to be obeyed to the letter. From the perspective of the New Testament, sabbath is the discipline of putting ourselves in the position of allowing Jesus to give us His rest. It applies not only to the chronological one day in seven we set aside from work, but also to the abiding rest we enjoy as a result of relationship with God.

In applying the principle of sabbath rest in our lives, we must be careful, as with all the disciplines, to exercise liberty. We are under no Old Testament obligation to observe the sabbath on a certain day (Saturday), or to refrain from gathering food or kindling a fire (Ex.

16:27-29; 35:3). Viewing sabbath rest in terms of do's and don'ts will only cause it to become more drudgery to us than work!

But neither does rest mean laying in bed all day doing nothing. Rest simply means ceasing from labor (Ex. 20:8-11; Deut. 5:12-15). Thus, the ensuing questions arise: "Can I cut the lawn, fix the car, or play sports on the sabbath?" Such questions are best answered by the individual. If the activity gives your body and mind a break from your normal everyday tasks, then by all means, go for it.

Some people find puttering around in the garage or trimming the rose bushes therapeutic and restful. Others find it relaxing to play a spirited game of touch football or volleyball, while still others are quite happy to sit under a tree and quietly read a book. What is important is that the activity relaxes you from the normal pace of your life.

The key to entering God's rest is allowing the Holy Spirit to show us practical ways in which we can physically and psychologically rest, and receive some "self-maintenance" in spirit, soul, and body.

I would add two cautions here in relation to the principle of sabbath rest. Firstly, we need to be careful that on our sabbath, we don't substitute one type of frenetic activity with another, feeding the workaholic inside us.

Secondly, in speaking about activities to partake in during a sabbath day, I don't mean to imply that they are a substitute for involvement in our local church. We are talking about a day of rest that may or may not coincide with Sunday and church. If we do make Sunday our sabbath rest day, we are obligated to make involvement in our local church part of the rest we enjoy on that day.

2—Receive the *promise* of sabbath rest. "Therefore, since the promise of entering his rest still stands, let us be careful that none of you be found to have fallen short of it" (Heb. 4:1).

The writer to the Hebrews goes on further to warn us that the promise of entering God's rest is only to those who combine faith with the promise. Thus, we will enter into God's rest to the degree that we desire it, and we will desire it to the degree that we believe it is His will for us.

We must also understand that we are moving in disobedience to God when we fail to enter into His rest. Western society has given us the idea that God is more pleased with frantic activity, good works, and neurotic worry than He is with our obedience. The passages in Hebrews chapters three and four regarding sabbath rest freely interchange the words *unbelief* and *disobedience*. God wants us to believe in and receive the promise of His rest as a test of our obedience.

Several years ago, I lived at a beach community called "Pleasure Point" in Santa Cruz, California, with my dog named Joshua. Joshua was one of the elite group of dogs known as "Pleasure Point stick dogs." He earned the distinction for his tenacity in chasing sticks.

I would take Joshua to the twenty-foot high cliff that overlooked the ocean at Pleasure Point, and throw a stick out into the surf. At breakneck speed, Joshua would charge down the dangerous cliff, plunge into the treacherous surf, retrieve the stick, clamber back up the cliff, drop the stick at my feet, and shake water all over me. Then, with fire in his heart, and determination in his eyes, Joshua would yelp, bark, whine, and whimper until I threw the stick back out into the ocean. He would then repeat the retrieval process.

One day, though, I decided to teach Joshua obedience. I threw the stick out into the ocean and said, "stay." Joshua was so upset that I thought his eyeballs would pop out of his head! He had been quite happy to obey me in the "work"—retrieving the stick—that he had grown to love, but sitting on top of that cliff with the stick floating in the surf below him, he was "laboring" to enter rest!

God's plan for us is like this; He throws the stick six times, then on the seventh time He says, "stay." It is just as disobedient for us to refuse to rest as it is to refuse to work.

Indeed, God was very serious about the importance of keeping the sabbath in the Old Testament. Death was the penalty He decreed for violating it (Ex. 31:14), primarily because He knew how beneficial resting on the sabbath was for us. Thus, we not only obey God, but do ourselves a favor when we receive His promise of rest.

3—See the *priority* of sabbath rest. By recognizing the principle and promise of rest, we then have the basis upon which we can make sabbath rest a priority in our lives. Depending upon the line of work in which we're involved, much of our time is scheduled for us by others, and we manage to fill up the rest of our time with our personal priorities. In my life, I have found that things such as time for God, family, rest, and self-maintenance tend to be squeezed out of my schedule by the demands of others, unless I make them a priority.

Thus, we must become ruthless with our time, scheduling sabbaths into our schedule weeks in advance. God is aware of the time pressures we all face. He knows that, at times, we simply must work incessantly without a break for days or weeks at a time. However, we must fight for ownership of our schedule, or we will eventually pay the price for being too busy.

Through trial and much error, I have learned that planning my schedule around my sabbaths is the best way to go. One of the hazards of being in full-time ministry is the nagging feeling that your work is never done. A builder can finish a building, a businessman can close a deal, and a salesman can make a sale, but it is impossible for a pastor to say that all the people in his congregation are fully discipled, spiritually fed, and cared for.

As the leader of a missionary training center, I can never say that we have trained and sent out enough workers. I must make sure my schedule serves me, lest I become a slave to the ministry in which I am involved. Scheduling regular sabbaths helps me to "close the loop" in my ministry.

My schedule often involves a lot of traveling, with the inevitable jet lag, customs and immigration hold-ups, and the hustle to get my bags off the baggage carousels. Other times, it involves an excessive amount of preaching, teaching, and counseling. Before a particularly hectic time, I will schedule a couple of sabbaths into my schedule before I leave, rather than waiting until I get back to take some time to recuperate. If I have a string of speaking engagements in the evenings while I'm home, I'll schedule some afternoon sabbaths to recharge my spiritual batteries and spend time with my family.

Someone has rightly said, "He who fails to plan is planning to fail." This is especially true of sabbaths. We must make them a priority, and plan them ahead of time into our schedule.

4—Establish a *practice* of regular "sabbathing." "There remains, then, a Sabbath-rest for the people of God" (Heb. 4:9).

As a young Christian, I was long on zeal and short on wisdom, adopting as my motto the words of an old saint, "Let me burn out for God." The embers of those profoundly spiritual words quickly lost their glow when I found out that the guy who uttered them died when he was 29!

As our society has transformed from an industrial society to an information society, the numbers of stress-induced illnesses, phobias, and various fatigue syndromes have reached near epidemic proportions. I know of a number of Christian leaders who have been put almost entirely out of action by the so-called Yuppie disease, the Epstein-Barr virus. It seems to thrive in bodies that are run down. An ever-increasing number of well-qualified pastors are quitting their churches to be involved in work they consider less stressful, such as denominational positions, chaplains for corporations, Bible school teachers, and the like. Thus, we must learn to monitor our minds and bodies and keep them far from (not teetering on the edge of) blow up, burn out, or break down.

To understand this more fully, let's return to the illustration of the marathon runner. A marathon runner will do several types of training in order to achieve his desired finish time. He will do some hill running to build up strength, some long-distance runs to develop endurance, and some short sprints to increase his speed.

The fourth crucial aspect of a marathon runner's conditioning is pacing—training your body to run at a consistent speed throughout a race. The old proverb says, "The race is not always to the swift, but to those who keep on running." How true this is in the Christian life. Far too many Christians are training for the 100 meter dash rather than the marathon, and as a result, they end up dropping out of the race. Through the use of the sabbath, we can learn to pace ourselves.

Another aspect of sabbath rest is taking "sabbath moments." A sabbath moment is the discipline of stopping to reflect, meditate, and wait upon God in the midst of the day.

By nature, I am an impetuous, impulsive, reactionary person, plagued by a malady called "foot in mouth disease." On many occasions, I have had to humble myself and ask forgiveness from someone at whom I had "popped off" during a moment of sarcasm, humor, or cynicism. Through learning to take sabbath moments—the spiritual equivalent of counting to ten—I have had less occasion to do or say something stupid.

During these sabbath moments, I simply wait, rest, and ask God to help me trust Him. I might say, "Lord, please give me a revelation right now of Your greatness and Your ability to work through me. Help me remember Your faithfulness." Or I may say nothing, and simply wait in silence. These times can be as short as thirty or forty seconds, but do wonders for the soul.

5—Enjoy the *productivity* of sabbath rest. "God saw all that he had made, and it was very good..." (Gen. 1:31).

There is a famous story about a time when Martin Luther was facing a very busy day. The work he needed to do required more time than he had at his disposal. He is recorded as remarking to one of his friends, "I have so much to do that I shall spend the first three hours in prayer!" The spiritual truth of this is hard for our natural minds to grasp. If we give God His due—first place in our lives—we will accomplish more, even though the time we actually have to work with is less.

Living in sabbath rest, whether it be one day in seven, or simply abiding in the sabbath rest promised by Jesus, is a statement of faith that we are ceasing from our work, just as God ceased from His (Heb. 4:10). We are declaring by our actions that our work will be even more productive when it is done God's way, which includes sabbath rest. This acknowledgement of our weakness enables God to work on our behalf.

Genesis reveals that after six days of creating, God took a break, or rested, in order to admire what He had created. Indeed, the text reveals that He took such a time after each day of creation. This suggests that another function of sabbath rest is to have time to appreciate and appraise what we have done during our period of work.

An interesting enigma arises here, similar to "Which came first, the chicken or the egg?" The enigma is: "Do we work in order to rest, or rest in order to work?" The Bible doesn't clearly say, but I suspect both are true. God divided night from day, and declared both to be "very good." Nighttime and rest are not necessarily evils to be endured in order to get more work done. To say that quality rest brings quality work is as true as the converse: quality work brings quality rest.

According to statistics, most industrial accidents happen in the hour before lunch and the hour before quitting time. This is when people are weary, needing rest to gather their strength. The same can be applied to the spiritual realm: the more physically or spiritually weary we are, the more vulnerable we are to satanic attack.

It is no accident that Satan tempted Jesus at the end of a forty-day fast. He knew when Jesus would be most vulnerable (Matt. 4:1-3). We cannot afford to be ignorant of the devil's devices (II Cor. 2:11). In those times when, through neglect or circumstances beyond our control, we become weary, we are the most vulnerable to spiritual attack.

Robert Murray McCheyne was a famous preacher who died at the age of twenty-nine. From his deathbed, he spoke these words, which should challenge us to develop the proper balance of work and rest in our lives: "God gave me a message to deliver and a horse to ride. Alas, I have killed the horse and now I cannot deliver the message." May God help us to receive His precious gift of sabbath rest, which He made for us, and allow that rest to do its renewing work in our lives.

Chapter Nine

Trainin' and Maintainin'

Discipline of the Body

"You're a thief and a robber!" This was not exactly what Pastor John expected to hear from a member of the congregation after the Sunday morning service, and especially not from a fellow pastor. He expected something more like, "That was a fine sermon," but not, "You're a thief and a robber." John recoiled a moment, then suggested that perhaps his fellow pastor's "radar" wasn't tracking correctly, because he certainly hadn't stolen anything since his conversion.

The fellow pastor responded, "You are a thief and a robber. You are robbing your congregation." John was again taken aback at this accusation, but the fellow pastor gave him no opportunity to answer.

"All the extra stress you're putting on your heart through the fatty foods you eat and your lack of exercise is robbing your congregation. If you don't do something about it, you'll end up robbing them of perhaps ten years of your life and ministry among them."

Pastor John, who weighed in at over 300 pounds, soon realized that this was a word from the Lord. He pondered it in his heart for a few days, then responded. He made himself accountable to others regarding his diet and fitness. He began watching what he ate, and started exercising regularly. Soon, Pastor John had shed over a hundred pounds.

Today, John looks great. He's trim and fit, and feels great. He is also a tremendous example to others of how God is concerned with our bodies, and gives us the grace to deal with them through physical discipline.

You may ask, "But isn't God more interested in the spiritual condition of my heart than in the physical condition of my body?" Yes, God is vitally interested in our spiritual well-being. He wants our hearts to be open and submitted to Him, but He is also concerned about the state of our bodies. When Paul says to Timothy, "Bodily exercise profits little" (I Tim. 4:8), he doesn't mean that we don't need to be concerned about our physical condition. All he is doing is contrasting for Timothy the eternal value of godliness as opposed to the temporal value of exercise. The "liberty" God gives us is not the liberty to use our body as a human garbage disposal, or to allow it to degenerate into a wasted wreck like a rusted, abandoned car, through lack of exercise.

God created us as a unit, an integrated whole: spirit, soul, and body. When we are born again, not only does God renew our heart, but our body becomes His dwelling place (I Cor. 6:19). This ought to cause us to have some concern over the maintenance of the house into which we have invited the Lord to live.

If the President of the United States were to come to stay with us, we would make sure everything was just right for him. We would provide him with the best of everything. We would certainly not expect him to sleep in a trashed, run-down house. He is the President, and worthy of the best we have to offer.

Why should we treat the Creator of the Universe any differently? He is infinitely worthy of the best we have to offer Him, which includes our bodies. Perhaps it's time some of us paid a little more attention to training and maintaining the temple of the Holy Spirit.

The Early Church was plagued by a heresy called "gnosticism" which, among other errors, taught that all matter, including our physical bodies, was evil, and that only "spirit" was good. Though much of this heresy has long since been purged from the Church, threads of it still remain.

Throughout church history, gnosticism has sparked some rather weird ideas about how to be holy. One third century mystic named Simeon Stylites, for instance, lived for thirty years atop a three-feet wide, sixty-feet high pillar. A ladder enabled his disciples to bring him food and remove his waste. When worms fell from the sores on his body, he would place them back and say to them, "Eat what God has given you." I understand that we should crucify the flesh, but come on, Simeon—lighten up!

Other monks from the Middle Ages hung for years suspended by iron shackles, took vows of absolute silence, whipped themselves until blood flowed, mixed their bread with sand, slept standing up, or slept lying down (on beds of nails, of course). Others deliberately wore coarse clothing to irritate their skin.

All this self-flagellation, wrongly described as "discipline," was done in order to conquer and subdue the "evil flesh," and thereby obtain a greater measure of spirituality. But irritated skin, beds of nails, iron shackles, sandy bread, and stone pillars don't sound much like the abundant life to me!

Thus, it is important that we have a good biblical understanding of our bodies, and the part they play in God's plan to make us like Him. The Bible does teach that we need to crucify the flesh, and that the "old man" has been crucified with Christ (Gal. 5:27; Rom. 6:6). However, neither of these terms is synonymous with our physical bodies.

Our bodies are the temple of the Holy Spirit (I Cor. 19), and are to be presented to God, a holy, living sacrifice (Rom. 12:1-2). When we sin, our bodies are the instrument that our heart uses to sin. Jesus said that the heart, or will, is where sin finds its origin (Matt. 15:18-19; James 1:13-15).

But our bodies can also be instruments of righteousness, and we are told not to let sin reign in our "mortal bodies" (Rom. 6:12-13). We can have holy hands (I Tim. 2:8), beautiful feet (Isa. 52:7; Rom. 10:15), hearing ears (Rev. 2:7), and clean lips (Isa. 6:7). It is also important to realize that Adam had a physical body before he fell into sin, and that Jesus had a body of flesh and blood. These facts should help us see that our bodies are not evil, or the origin of evil.

Eating to live, or living to eat?

In light of the above, it makes good sense that we concern ourselves with the state of our body. While bearing in mind that the "...kingdom of God is not a matter of eating and drinking..." (Rom. 14:17), and that "...food does not bring us near to God..." (I Cor. 8:8), it would do us well to evaluate our diet. This is true, especially in light of our responsibility to be good stewards of what God has given us, in this case, our bodies.

Are we are eating in order to live, or living in order to eat? Is your dietary intake serving your body, or is your body merely serving your appetite?

Since our bodies have been "purchased" by God, they are His possession, and we need to be good stewards over what He has given us. The following two guidelines should help guide us as we seek to discipline ourselves in this area of our diet, and exercise stewardship over our bodies.

1—Examine yourself, not others (II Cor. 13:5; Matt. 7:1; James 4:11-12). The Bible teaches that what we eat and drink is a matter of individual conscience as enlightened by the Holy Spirit (I Cor. 8; 10:23-31; Rom. 14:1-10). Thus, we have no right to judge and condemn others because of their diet. How often I have seen Christians be very critical of those who smoke, quoting I Corinthians 6:19 as a proof text, while at the same time they are bombarding their stomach, pancreas, and heart with daily overdoses of caffeine, sugar, and cholesterol.

Tragically, I have also encountered a number of overweight people who have been deeply wounded by the way others judged them to be unspiritual without having the facts. Many of these people had a chemical imbalance or a glandular malfunction at the root of their weight problem. Even if there is no physiological problem, we still have no right to judge.

If God is dealing with you about how much sugar you daily put into your body, then be obedient to Him, but don't criticize others to whom God may not be speaking about sugar. There are many complex factors that contribute to the various eating disorders (anorexia, bulimia, obesity, and the like). We must make sure that we are not contributing, through a critical spirit, to the pain of someone afflicted with one of these disorders.

2—Eat to live, don't live to eat. "'Everything is permissible for me'—but not everything is beneficial. 'Everything is permissible for me'—but I will not be mastered by anything" (I Cor. 6:12).

The whole area of nutrition is not so much an issue of God's legal requirements on us as it is a matter of stewardship. Are we treating the body God has given us with a "disciplined liberty" that guards us from the extremes of health food fanaticism on the one hand, and "junk food junky-ism" on the other?

We have the liberty to enjoy food. God gave us taste buds for a reason. However, keep in mind Peter's warning that "...a man is a slave to whatever has mastered him" (II Pet. 2:19). Solomon, reflecting upon life "under the sun," observed that, "All man's efforts are for his mouth, yet his appetite is never satisfied" (Ecc. 6:7). Throughout the Bible, we are warned that gluttony is a work of the flesh that needs to be crucified (Deut. 21:20; Prov. 23:1-3,21; Phil. 3:19; Gal. 5:24). While keeping in mind Paul's admonition about end-time false teachers who will command us to "...abstain from certain foods, which God created to be received with thanksgiving by those who believe and who know the truth" (I Tim. 4:1-5), we should, nonetheless, ask God for the wisdom and common sense to let nutrition and health guide our decisions regarding diet.

Some of us may be serving the Lord in places where the control over our diet is out of our hands, or where, for economic reasons, we are deprived of the opportunity to choose healthy food. In these situations, God gives us grace, and is able supernaturally to keep us healthy.

Our responsibility before God, though, is to be good stewards over the bodies with which He has entrusted us. In this, He is willing to help us live up to the light that both our conscience and His Spirit give us (I Cor. 10:23-31). If, however, your confession is that you can't live without certain foods, then you are probably in bondage to that food.

Once, after I presented a slide show on the needs of world missions, a young lady came up to me and volunteered to go overseas as a missionary. She was excited and enthusiastic about the prospects, until she found out that most people in Asia eat white rice rather than brown rice. This young lady considered brown rice essential to her diet. As a result, she allowed brown rice to quench her "call" to serve God overseas as a missionary. She was in bondage to brown rice, a point that I lovingly tried to explain to her. In addition,

I believe she was dangerously close to idolatry, putting her body above the call of God.

Junk food or health food, it matters not. Each one will keep us from God's highest for our life if our god is our belly (Phil. 3:19). The key is obedience and moderation, not hypocrisy and bondage.

Exercise

An equally important factor in the area of bodily discipline is physical exercise. We are told that we have been "purchased" by Christ on the cross and are, therefore, to "...glorify God in your body..." (I Cor. 6:20 KJV). Our body is the instrument God has given each of us, through which to show forth His glory during our short sojourn on planet earth.

Our commitment to physical exercise shows our desire to maintain the temple in which we have invited Christ to come and live. No one in his right mind would purchase a new car, then neglect to do regular maintenance or check the water, oil, and brake fluid levels. Such inattention would soon destroy the effectiveness of the car. Through diet and exercise, we maintain our bodies. Failure to pay proper attention to both of these areas will ultimately destroy our body's effectiveness.

The Bible tells us that health and living a long life are good things, and blessings from God (I Pet. 3:10-12). Someone has said that we are living too short and dying too long. Both, in many cases, can be avoided.

The benefits of exercise are legion, both psychologically and physically. Not only will we feel better in our minds, but we also will begin to experience less fatigue, sleep better, lose weight, look better, decrease the risk of heart disease (the #1 killer), strengthen our immune system, and increase the probability of living a long life.

Exercise physiologists have discovered what has been termed the "runner's high," which is a euphoric feeling which runners experience through sustained cardiovascular exercise. As the pulse is sped up through exercise, endorphins are released into the brain, and they simply make the person feel good.

Medical experts tell us that the best exercise is that which gives us a sustained increase in our heart rate for 20-30 minutes at a time. They say that we should do this type of exercise a bare minimum of four times a week. There are a number of sports activities to provide this type of exercise. The most popular, and easiest to do consistently and cheerfully, are running, brisk walking, swimming, cycling, and rowing. Any one of these is great exercise, can be done alone, and are not expensive. Tennis, racquetball, volleyball, and other fast-moving sports also provide the same heart rate increase, but are sometimes more difficult to do consistently, because of the need for other people to be involved with us.

The important thing is to be consistent and enjoy the sport in which we're involved. God wants us to enjoy life (I Tim. 6:17; John 10:10) and celebrate the fact that He has made us physical beings. Just as He has given us taste buds to enjoy food, and a human spirit to enjoy Him, He has also given us a body with which we can enjoy His creation.

There will be some sports toward which you naturally gravitate, and others which will grow on you as time goes by. I began long-distance running when I was thirteen years old, simply because I was too small for football. I've run over 20,000 miles since then, and I still love to run! I even believe God is pleased that there is something I enjoy in this world.

As Eric Liddel said to his sister, Jenny, in the movie *Chariots of Fire*, "God made me for a purpose, and He made me fast, and when I run, I can feel His pleasure."

Dallas Willard, in his book *The Spirit of the Disciples*, says that unfortunately, "...the One who came to give abundance of life is commonly thought of as a cosmic stuffed shirt, whose excessive 'spirituality' probably did not allow him normal bodily functions and certainly would not permit him to throw a frisbee or tackle someone in a football game."

By our inattention to diet and exercise, we may be robbing God and the world of the only precious gift we have to offer—our lives. Instead of wasting our bodies, let's offer them to God as living, vibrant, healthy, and fit sacrifices (Rom. 12:1). If it is within your power to do this, then do it, and trust Him to make up the difference when you can't.

Chapter Ten

Go for the Gold!

As you move along the tree-lined boulevard, you can feel the change within. Exhaustion turns to euphoria. Your muscles pump hard with a surge of newfound energy. The crowd lining the boulevard applauds as you make your way along.

You round a corner, then you see the stadium, rising high and stark against a crystal sky. Your legs unconsciously start picking up the pace as you approach. The throng of spectators grows. They crane to catch a glimpse of you, and talk excitedly among themselves. It's closer now.

Your eyes blink in the shadows of the tunnel leading into the stadium. Then the sunlight reappears at the end of the darkness. You see the crowd in the bleachers, which seem to climb upward to infinity. As you step into the sunlight again, the people jump to their feet, and erupt into cheering. You're inside the stadium now, and you can feel the sound of the crowd vibrate through your body. Only one lap to go.

Your slumping body pulls itself erect. Your legs begin pumping faster and faster, fueled by the energy of the moment. One more lap. No one in sight. No one to challenge you. You know it's yours, but still your legs won't slow down. You don't just want to finish, but you want to finish strong.

Two hundred meters to go. One hundred. Fifty. Your legs are pumping like a sprinter's. You are carried on the waves of excitement surrounding you. Ten meters. Five. Two.

Then you feel it—the white ribbon stretched across your chest, then snapped by your arms. You've done it! You've finished the course.

The cheering grows louder and louder, until you think the stadium will shatter with the sound. You're exhausted. Your body wants to lay down, rest, sleep, dance, jump, sing, and shout with joy, all at the same time. People crowd around to shake your hand and pat you on the back. The track is covered with the cables connecting the eyes of TV cameras with their studios. A sea of people with plastic "Press" badges vie for your comments. The lenses from what seem a million cameras jostle to keep you in focus. The eyes of the world are upon you. This is your moment!

Slowly, the mayhem of the moment recedes. Other runners are crossing the finish line, and are being congratulated. But you're the one who crossed it first. This race belongs to you.

Finally, all the runners have finished. Your pulse has returned to normal. You know you're tired, but you feel exhilarated. The crowd quiets.

You hear the crackle of the sound system, then the announcer's voice calling your name. You step up to the winner's platform, standing tall. The king of the country where the games are being held steps forward. He takes the medal from the velvet cushion carried by a young attendant. You lean over, bowing your head, and the King places the ribbon around your neck. As you straighten up, he shakes your hand and offers a few words of congratulation.

You stand erect to acknowledge the cheers of the crowd. As you do, you can feel the medal bobbing against your chest. You wrap your fingers around it.

This is what you trained for. This is the reward for all your hours of training. This is your reward for all the good things you had to cut from your schedule in order to have the necessary time for training. This is your reward for not giving up the first time you hit The Wall. Everything is worth it, when measured against this prize—the gold medal that hangs around your neck. Nothing could be greater than this moment. It's your moment, and you savor it, oblivious to all else.

Hebrews 12:1-3 contains a similar illustration: "Therefore, since we are surrounded by such a great cloud of witnesses, let us throw off everything that hinders and the sin that so easily entangles, and let us run with perseverance the race marked out for us. Let us fix our eyes on Jesus, the author and perfecter of our faith, who for the joy set before him endured the cross, scorning its shame, and sat down at the right hand of the throne of God. Consider him who endured such opposition from sinful men, so that you will not grow weary and lose heart."

The prize for successfully completing the Christian life awaits you. Are you ready to rise to the challenge and do whatever is necessary in order to cross the finish line and claim your prize? Are you going to be knocked out of the Christian life the first time you encounter The Wall? Or are you going to get up and discipline and train yourself, so that the next time you encounter The Wall, you'll press right on through it?

The prize is yours. All you have to do is choose. Once you have made the choice, you must discipline and train yourself so you will have the staying power you need.

May no one ever have to ask of us what Paul had to ask of the Galatians: "You were running a good race. Who cut in on you and kept you from obeying the truth?" (Gal. 5:7)

Instead, may these words of Paul be our testimony: "I press on toward the goal to win the prize for which God has called me heavenward in Christ Jesus" (Phil. 3:14). "However, I consider my life worth nothing to me, if only I may finish the race and complete the task the Lord Jesus has given me..." (Acts 20:24).

It's time to get our eyes on the prize and *go for the gold!*

Appendix I

Principles of Bible Interpretation

Comparing Scripture with Scripture. For the most part, the Bible is a self-explaining volume. Before consulting commentaries or other helps, simply research all the Bible has to say on a given subject. This will help distinguish between what the Bible records and what it approves, what it prescribes and what it describes. This guards against the danger of building a doctrine on an isolated passage without at least two or three passages that witness to it.

The principle of first mention. Always keep in mind the first time a given subject is mentioned in the Bible. It will often shed light on subsequent passages.

The principle of context. Every statement in the Bible has a historical and cultural setting (context), which helps determine its meaning. Taken at face value, with no regard for context, a verse such as II John 10 would be taken to mean that you could never invite a non-Christian into your house. Likewise, I Corinthians 11 would require women to wear a head covering every time they went to church.

We must also consider the grammatical context. Reading the paragraph before and after the text in question will aid in this regard. Without this caution, we could accuse David of atheism: "There is no God" (Ps. 14:1) and homosexuality (I Sam. 21:41). Someone has said, "A text without a context is a pretext."

Understanding various "genres" (kinds) of biblical literature. We must understand that there are many ways God expresses Himself in the Bible. We see, for example, that the poetic books are different from the Old Testament narratives or the gospels, that Jesus' parables are not literal accounts of history, or that there is a difference between a Bible command and a Bible example.

Understanding various forms of biblical language. There is figurative language (Jesus said he was a light, a door, and a vine—John 8, 10, 15), hyperbole (eye-plucking, hand-severing—Matt. 5:29-30), allegory (Gal. 4:21-31), anthropomorphism (Ps. 44:3; Isa. 59:1), symbolism (Daniel and Revelation), and many other types of language which the Holy Spirit used as He inspired the writers of the Bible.

The principle of literal meaning. In general, a text should be taken literally, unless the context, language, or kind of literature suggests otherwise. Also, obscure passages should be interpreted in light of the clear ones.

Appendix II

Recommended Books

Discipline

The Disciplined Life; Richard Shelly Taylor, Bethany House (1962).

The Spirit of the Disciplines; Dallas Willard, Harper & Row (1988)

Celebration of Discipline; Richard Foster, Harper & Row (1978)

Ordering Your Private World; Gordon MacDonald, Oliver-Nelson (1984)

Restoring Your Spiritual Passion; Gordon MacDonald, Oliver-Nelson (1986)

Prayer Life

The Kneeling Christian; An Unknown Christian, Zondervan

The writings of E.M. Bounds, Dick Eastman, David Bryant, or Leonard Ravenhill.

Bible Study

How to Read the Bible For All Its Worth; Fee & Stuart, Zondervan (1982)

A Guide to Understanding the Bible; Josh McDowell, Here's Life Publishers

ADDITIONAL BOOKS AND TAPES FROM DANNY LEHMANN

Books:
• *Bringin 'Em Back Alive,* by Danny Lehmann
Evangelism... Witnessing... Missions...If these words strike fear in your heart, then this book is for you! Through practical illustrations, personal examples, and clear concise teaching, Danny Lehmann encourages and challenges Christians to get involved in the Great Commission. Based on experience and rooted in Scripture, **BRINGIN 'EM BACK ALIVE** provides the ammunition you need to reach your world for Jesus.

• *The Facts of Life*
A 16 page Gospel booklet presenting the Gospel of Jesus Christ, designed to help you in sharing your faith.
(4 color cover)

Audio Cassettes
• *Bringin 'Em Back Alive* - tape album
Six teaching tapes on developing a lifestyle of evangelism.

• *Before You Hit the Wall* - tape album
Six teaching tapes on developing a lifestyle of discipline.

For information on these items, write to:
Danny Lehmann
Youth With A Mission
P.O. Box 61700
Honolulu, Hawaii 96839 USA

Video Cassettes
• *Before You Hit the Wall*
A six hour video teaching series on **BEFORE YOU HIT THE WALL**

• *Bringin 'Em Back Alive*
A eight hour video teaching series on **BRINGIN 'EM BACK ALIVE**

Both video series are available from:
University of the Nations Video
75-5851 Kuakini Highway
Kailua-Kona, Hawaii 96740 USA

LIFE-CHANGING BOOKS AND CASSETTES FROM YOUTH WITH A MISSION

YWAM Books:

- *Is That Really You God?*, by Loren Cunningham ($6.95) The exciting history of Youth With A Mission. In this book you see how an ordinary man who was committed to hearing God and obeying Him, became the founder of an extraordinary mission organization. An adventure in hearing and obeying the voice of God.

- *Anchor in the Storm*, by Helen Applegate ($6.95) The gripping true story of how Helen and her husband Ben, former captain of the mercy ship, M/V Anastasis, persevered through insurmountable odds to hold on to their dream to serve God on the high seas.

- *Before You Hit the Wall*, by Danny Lehmann ($6.95) The Christian life is likened unto the training of the marathon runner. This practical book shows how the disciplined life is not only attainable but enjoyable. It will equip you to "run" your spiritual race victoriously.

- *Daring to Live on the Edge: The Adventure of Faith and Finances*, by Loren Cunningham ($7.95) A compelling, fresh look at the subject of faith and finances by one of America's premier missions statesmen. This book will challenge and equip all who want to obey God's call, but who wonder where the money will come from.

- *The Father Heart of God*, by Floyd McClung ($5.95) Floyd, Executive Director of YWAM, shares how to know God as a loving, caring Father and a healer of our hurts.

- *Intimate Friendship with God*, by Joy Dawson ($6.95) Keys to knowing, obeying, and loving God by this dynamic teacher.

- *Leadership for the 21st Century*, by Ron Boehme ($7.95) At the close of the century, how will you lead? A great book with the goal of changing the nations through the power of serving.

- *Learning to Love People You Don't Like*, by Floyd McClung ($6.95) Knowing that biblical unity is not always easy, this book shares keys for loving others, even when it is hard.

- *Living on the Devil's Doorstep*, by Floyd McClung ($8.95) Join Floyd and his wife, Sally, in urban missions with YWAM, as they live first in a hippie hotel in Kabul, Afghanistan, and then next door to prostitutes, pimps, drug dealers, and homosexuals in Amsterdam, Holland.

- *Personal Prayer Diary-Daily Planner* ($11.95) What you get: quiet time journal, daily agenda, weekly goals, systematic Scripture readings, unreached people groups to pray for, prayer journal, concise teaching section, 9 pages of maps, and much more.

- *Some of the Ways of God in Healing*, by Joy Dawson ($6.95) All-out integrity from the author in the probing of scripture on the subject. Joy is ruthless in her pursuit of truth.

- *Spiritual Warfare for Every Christian*, by Dean Sherman ($6.95) Spiritual Warfare requires Spirit-controlled thinking and attitudes. Dean delivers a no-nonsense, practical approach to living in victory.

- *Streetwise*, by John Goodfellow ($6.95) John's pursuit of freedom only brought him deeper into the web of bondage. A compelling story of God's pursuit of one man and how He gave him true freedom.

- *Taking Our Cities for God*, by John Dawson (7.95) New bestseller on how to break spiritual strongholds. John Dawson gives you the strategies and tactics for taking your cities.

- *Target Earth*, by University of the Nations/Global Mapping Int'l ($27.95) This 170 page, full color atlas is filled with facts, maps, and articles by some fifty contributors.

- *Walls of My Heart*, by Dr. Bruce Thompson ($8.95) Dr. Bruce's popular teaching, now in book form, deals with the wounds and hurts that we all receive, and how to receive biblical healing.

- *We Cannot but Tell*, by Ross Tooley ($6.95) How to evangelize with love and compassion. Great for group studies as well as personal growth. Learn to reach out from your heart.

- *Winning, God's Way*, by Loren Cunningham ($6.95) Winning comes through laying down your life. This book gives the reader a look at the Cunningham's personal struggles and victories. A classic teaching of YWAM.

YWAM Tape Albums:

- "Let's Turn the World Around," by Loren Cunningham. An album of 6 audio cassettes ($24.95) Loren Cunningham founder of Youth With A Mission lays the basis for effectively changing the world with the Gospel.

- "Relationships," by Dean Sherman. An album of 6 audio cassettes ($24.95) Dean challenges us to live and walk in right relationships.

- "Spiritual Warfare," by Dean Sherman. An album of 12 audio cassettes ($39.95) Dean explores the many dynamics and strategies of spiritual warfare.

For a complete catalog of books and cassettes, write to the address below. To order any of the above listed books, write the title and quantity desired and send with the amount in US dollars.

FREE shipping at book rate with your order from this book.

Youth With A Mission Books
P.O. Box 55787
Seattle, WA 98155 USA
Tel. (206) 771-1153